CONTESTED POLICY

Al Filo: Mexican American Studies Series
Series Editor Roberto R. Calderón, University of North Texas.

Al Filo: Mexican American Studies Series will be interdisciplinary but will exclude literary studies, fiction, and poetry. Instead, the Series will pursue publishing titles in the areas of history and culture. The Mexican American experience in the Southwest, and especially Texas, will be emphasized, but also welcome for consideration are studies of issues in U.S.-Mexico border studies and titles covering areas in the United States outside of the Southwest. The Series will cast a wide chronological approach from colonial times to the present day, but most titles will discuss topics set in the nineteenth and twentieth centuries. Submissions for the Series will be welcomed primarily from historians but also from anthropologists, sociologists, political scientists, and those who practice in fine arts and other disciplines. Original monographs and studies will be favored, but anthologies, edited documentary volumes, studies based on oral history, and autobiographies will also be considered for the Series. Manuscripts for the Series are invited for consideration.

CONTESTED POLICY

The Rise and

Fall of Federal

Bilingual Education

in the United States

1960–2001

Guadalupe San Miguel, Jr.

Number 1 in the Al Filo: Mexican American Studies Series

University of North Texas Press
Denton, Texas

10 9 8 7 6 5 4 3 2 1

Permissions:
University of North Texas Press
P.O. Box 311336
Denton, TX 76203-1336

The paper used in this book meets the minimum requirements of the
American National Standard for Permanence of Paper for Printed Library
Materials, z39.48.1984. Binding materials have been chosen for durability.

Library of Congress Cataloging-in-Publication Data

San Miguel, Guadalupe, 1950–
  Contested policy : the rise and fall of federal bilingual education in
the United States, 1960-2001 / Guadalupe San Miguel, Jr.
    p. cm. — (Al filo ; no. 1)
Includes bibliographical references.
  ISBN 1-57441-171-3 (cloth : alk. paper)
  1. Mexican Americans—Education—History—20th century. 2. Education,
Bilingual—United States—History—20th century. 3. Educational
equalization—United States—History—20th century. I. Title. II.
Series.
LC2683.S36 2003
370.117'0973—dc22
                                2003020875

*Contested Policy: The Rise and Fall of Federal Bilingual Education in the United States,
1960–2001* is Number 1 in the Al Filo: Mexican American Studies Series

Text design by Carol Sawyer of Rose Design

CONTENTS

ACKNOWLEDGMENTS

I would like to thank my colleagues in the history department of the University of Houston and in the Center for Mexican American Studies for their encouragement and resources, and for granting me much needed public spaces to develop the ideas for this book. Although this project began in the 1980s, their moral and financial support became crucial in the final phase of its completion.

I would also like to thank my beautiful wife, Alicia, for all her insightful comments relating to bilingual education. Her teaching experiences in this program and her knowledge of the theory of bilingual education added immensely to my understanding of the politics of formulating and implementing educational policy.

Finally, *miles de besos y abrazos* (thousands of kisses and hugs) go to my kids (Ysaura, Pablo, and Gabriel) for putting up with my changing moods during these past few years as I completed the manuscript.

To all of these individuals and to the many others who over the years have questioned, supported, and prodded me in this effort *muchísimas gracias* (many thanks).

INTRODUCTION

Bilingual education is one of the most contentious and misunderstood educational programs in the United States because it raises significant questions about national identity, federalism, power, ethnicity, and pedagogy. It raises questions about how one defines an American in general and the role of ethnicity in American life in particular. It also raises questions about relations between federal, state, and local governments and between majority and minority groups. Finally, it raises questions about instructional methodologies and their relationship to immigrant and native children. How do you teach immigrant children in general and how do you teach English to them in particular? Also, how do you teach foreign languages to American children in the elementary and secondary grades?

Because of these issues, federal bilingual education policy over the last three and a half decades has had a turbulent and contested history. The contested nature of bilingual education is reflected in its uneven development and in the inconsistent pattern of popular support. In the 1960s and 1970s, bilingual education policy increasingly favored the use of non-English languages and cultures. By the latter part of the 1980s and 1990s, however, non-English languages and cultures played a small and decreasing role in this policy. In the early years, a variety of federal, state, and local agencies, educational groups, and lay people supported bilingual education. This support visibly decreased by the 1990s.

The changes in bilingual education, in general, were the result of several forces, including litigation, legislation, a changing political context, and activism on the part of contending groups with competing notions of ethnicity, assimilation, empowerment, and pedagogy. Of particular importance in its evolution was the role played by two major contending groups: the opponents and the proponents of bilingual education.

The latter group, comprised of language specialists, Mexican-American activists, newly enfranchised civil rights advocates, language minorities, intellectuals, professional educators, teachers, students, and others, was ideologically opposed to the assimilationist philosophy that underlay the subtractive and conformist policies and practices in the schools. Proponents were also opposed to the structural exclusion and institutional discrimination against racialized groups, and to limited school reform.

The proponents not only articulated oppositional ideologies, structures, and policies, they also proposed alternative ones aimed at supporting cultural and linguistic pluralism, a strong federal role, ethnic minority political empowerment, and significant school change. More specifically, they supported perspectives that viewed cultural resurgence as the key to minority academic and socioeconomic success and significant education reform as an instrument of political empowerment.

These varied individuals with their multiple perspectives collectively challenged the cultural and political hegemony of the dominant groups by promoting significant educational reforms and by supporting the re-introduction of language, culture, and community into the public schools. Specific reforms were proposed by activists including the elimination of the English-only laws, the enactment of federal and state legislation supporting the use of non-English languages in the conduct and operation of public institutions, especially the schools, and the hiring of minority language administrators and teachers.

The opponents of bilingual education, comprised at different points in time of conservative journalists, politicians, federal bureaucrats, Anglo parent groups, school officials, administrators, and special interest groups such as U.S. English, favored assimilationism, the structural exclusion of and discrimination against ethnic minorities, and limited school reform. These individuals and groups were not organized until the late 1970s. In the late 1960s and 1970s, in fact, there was no active or organized opposition to bilingual education although there was significant passive resistance to the use of non-English languages in the schools and to the use of schools as instruments of minority empowerment. After 1978, however, this group coalesced around several key ideas that included ideological opposition to pluralism, an "intrusive" federal role, minority empowerment, significant language-based school reform, and primary language instruction in public education. The underlying tensions and differences between these contending groups, I argue, led to the development of contested school policy over the years.

The following pages provide only a brief sketch of the origins, evolution, and consequences of federal bilingual education policy during the years from 1960 to 2001. They also describe and explain the role played by the contending groups of supporters and opponents in its development. Much more research needs to be done on the details of this history and on those who shaped this policy. For now, only the outlines of the major developments will be described.

Additionally, this book includes an extended bibliographic essay of the sources written from 1960 to 2001 that can be used to do an in-depth history of this policy. This essay is organized into the three major stages of the policy-making cycle as discussed by James E. Anderson: the formation, implementation, and impact or evaluation stages. These three stages comprise one policy-making cycle. Bilingual education policy has gone through six major policy cycles since it was first enacted. These three stages occurred within each policy cycle and repeated themselves in the following ones. The first policy cycle for the federal bilingual education act occurred between 1965 and 1974. It ended with the reauthorization of the bilingual bill in the latter year. Since 1974, this bill has been reauthorized five additional times: 1978, 1984, 1988, 1994, and 2001. Federal bilingual education policy, therefore, has gone through six policy cycles. The extended essay discusses pertinent literature related to each aspect of these six policy cycles.[1]

This book, then, has two parts. The first part is a brief interpretation of the historical origins and evolution of federal bilingual education from 1960 to 2001. The second part is an extended bibliographic essay of materials pertinent to the history of federal bilingual education in the U.S.

The first part contains an introduction, four chapters, and a conclusion. The first chapter describes the political climate of the 1960s and how the proponents of bilingual education utilized the swirl of ideas associated with this period to develop the arguments in support of the first Bilingual Education Act of 1968. It also describes the major events leading up to the formulation and enactment of this bill. Chapter Two focuses on the expansion and transformation of federal bilingual education policy from a minor piece of legislation to a significant piece of school reform. Chapter Three provides an explanation of the emergence of opposition to bilingual education and the ideological and policy changes it sought. The following chapter addresses the resurgence of opposition to bilingual education in the latter part of the 1990s and its success in repealing and replacing this bill with an English-only piece of legislation. The conclusion discusses the major findings of this study.

The second part contains the extended bibliography essay of materials pertinent to the history of bilingual education.

NOTES

1. James E. Anderson, *Public Policy-making* (New York: Praeger, 1975).

CHAPTER 1

ORIGINS OF FEDERAL BILINGUAL EDUCATION POLICY

Bilingual education is not a new phenomenon. It has existed in various forms since this nation's founding. The use of non-English languages as well as the use of two or more languages to teach academic subjects to individuals in the elementary, secondary, or post-secondary grades has been supported, tolerated, or sanctioned by public and parochial school officials since the 1600s.[1] For the most part, local or state officials made these language decisions. The federal government rarely legislated language choice, although it discouraged the use of non-English languages in American life, especially in the territories and among certain immigrant and racial minority groups.[2] The tradition of refraining from taking official action related to language policies in general or school language policies in particular ended in 1968. In this year, the U.S. Congress passed the Bilingual Education Act.[3] Why and how this occurred is the emphasis of this chapter.

Professional educators and language specialists initiated the contemporary push for federal bilingual education policy in the early part of the decade, but newly enfranchised Chicano/a activists, civil rights groups, and educational activists soon joined them. Although activist educators, language specialists, ethnic minorities, and others were crucial in the origins of bilingual education policy, several significant contextual factors influenced their ideas and approaches. Among the most important of these during the first half of the 1960s were bilingual research findings, the civil rights movement, federal social legislation and the emerging Chicano and Chicana Movement. These contextual forces brought to light questions about national identity, the federal role in school change, power, and pedagogy, and eventually contributed to the enactment of the federal Bilingual Education Act of 1968.

CONTEXTUAL FACTORS

Research on bilingualism—i.e., on the impact and extent of "non-English languages" in American society—began to influence many of the arguments that advocates would use to support bilingual education policy. This new research questioned two prominent myths in education: the myth of the negative impact of bilingualism on intelligence and on academic achievement and the myth of the declining significance of ethnicity in American life as implied by the melting pot theory of assimilation.

Research on Bilingualism

Since the 1920s, research on intelligence and achievement had indicated that bilingualism was an obstacle to success. This research showed a negative relationship between dual language capabilities and intelligence. However, in the early 1960s a gradual shift occurred in this literature. Scholars found that bilingualism was an asset to learning in the schools and that it played a positive role in intelligence.[4] More specifically, they found that bilingual children were either equal to or superior to monolinguals on intelligence tests and in other areas of language usage.[5]

Bilingual research studies also questioned the myth of underachievement based on language barriers. These new studies indicated that, in conjunction with other reforms, "non-English" or native language instruction could improve school achievement in general, rather than retard it.[6] These studies also indicated that bilingualism could improve second language acquisition in particular. One such study, for example, found that Spanish-speaking children instructed bilingually tended to perform as well in English language skills and in the content areas as comparable students taught only in English. At the same time, these children were developing language skills in Spanish. Anglo students in bilingual programs were not adversely affected in their English language development and in the content subjects, and were learning a second language, Spanish.[7]

This new research likewise raised questions about assimilation. Traditional theory had argued that ethnicity in general and ethnic minority languages and cultures in particular would disappear over time as a result of ethnic group assimilation into American life. Research on bilingualism, however, indicated that certain minority groups in the United States maintained their language abilities and cultural identity over time.[8] Bilingualism and biculturalism, in other words, were not disappearing but being maintained and, in some cases, increasing. Much of this bilingualism was due to the language maintenance among the French-speaking groups in the Northeast and the Spanish-speaking population in the Southwest. [9]

This new bilingual research reinforced the work of scholars such as Nathan Glazer and Daniel Moynihan. These two noted scholars of the immigrant experience based their research on ethnic and immigrant groups in New York City and argued that people maintained their cultural identities and felt close affiliation to those of the same group. According to them, cultural and linguistic pluralism was a much more common phenomenon than previously assumed. More specifically, ethnic and language minority groups were not melting and ethnicity was not declining as rapidly as many scholars had believed. The melting pot, in other words, was a myth.[10]

Civil Rights Movement

Domestic concerns, especially the growth of the civil rights movements and the passage of the War on Poverty legislation in the early 1960s, focused increased attention on the problems experienced by people of color living in poverty and the role that the federal government could play in resolving these issues.

The growing strength of the black civil rights movement, that is, the struggle for voting rights, equal employment, and an end to segregation in public facilities, as well as the enactment of civil rights policies, focused attention on the presence of racial discrimination in American life. The

civil rights movement also suggested new means for eliminating discriminatory policies and practices, including the use of protest, demonstrations, pickets, and increased federal involvement.[11]

Language scholars and ethnic minority activists strongly supported
the civil rights movement. They, however, began to argue that discrimination was not simply based on race but on other factors such as
national origin, religion, and gender. In the case of Spanish-speaking
children and with respect to bilingual education arguments, civil rights
leaders and educators began to emphasize the impact and significance of
discrimination based on language and culture. This type of discrimination, many activists and scholars argued, negatively impacted the school
achievement of Mexican Americans in particular and language minority
children in general.[12]

These activists also began to argue that the federal government had a
responsibility for overcoming all forms of discrimination. Like racial discrimination, many of them noted, inequitable treatment on the basis of
language and culture could be eliminated in the schools with the support
of the federal government.

Social Legislation

The enactment of poverty legislation also influenced the arguments
for bilingual education. This type of legislation led to a renewed consideration of poverty and educational underachievement especially among
language minority groups in general and Spanish speaking minority
children in particular. It also encouraged individuals to look for a stronger
federal role in eliminating poverty.

The federal government discovered poverty in the early 1960s and
declared war on it. Education became instrumental in winning this war
on poverty. With respect to public education, Congress enacted two
major pieces of legislation aimed at developing social and educational
programs to meet this federal goal: the Economic Opportunity Act of
1964 and the Elementary and Secondary Education Act of 1965. The former, among other things, required the involvement of poor parents in
the development and implementation of federal programs. The latter

provided funds to public schools and led to a renewed emphasis on eliminating poverty in the ghettos and barrios through education.[13]

The War on Poverty legislation and increased federal involvement in education encouraged scholars to focus on the factors impacting school performance among poor children of color residing in ghettos, barrios, and reservations. Those interested in the education of Latino children emphasized the impact that structural exclusion of the community and discriminatory school policies such as no-Spanish speaking rules and English-only laws had on the underachievement of poor Spanish-speaking children. Structural exclusion and institutional discrimination, they argued, led to the lowering of self-esteem and eventual school failure of language minority students.[14]

Other activists, especially language specialists, argued that English-only laws and practices led to the waste of necessary national language resources that could benefit the country.[15]

The ultimate result of these debates was to shift the blame for underachievement from minority children and their language and culture to larger institutional and structural forces, especially discriminatory school policies.

Activists and Cultural Pluralism

Finally, the emerging Chicano and Chicana movement became an important ingredient in the rationale for bilingual education. The activists of the 1960s, among other things, were ideologically opposed to assimilation, cultural repression, and Anglo hegemony in the public schools. They strongly opposed assimilation and viewed themselves as being culturally victimized and structurally excluded by the dominant society and its institutions, including the schools. They also viewed themselves as being controlled by an Anglo political and economic elite not interested in their academic or societal progress. For most activists of this period, political empowerment and cultural identity were necessary for minority academic and socioeconomic progress.[16]

The activists of the 1960s and early 1970s, in conjunction with others, challenged the cultural and political hegemony of the dominant groups and promoted significant educational reforms, including bilingual education. They supported bilingual education for at least four reasons. First, they viewed this program as a strategy for the structural inclusion of those elements that had been historically excluded from the schools in the past: the Spanish language, Mexican culture, and the Mexican origin community.[17] Second, many activists viewed bilingual education as "a vehicle for institutional change."[18] Although a few of them initially were suspicious of bilingual education,[19] most came to believe that the enactment of bilingual language policies could lead to the elimination of discriminatory school policies and practices and to significant changes in assimilationist curricular policies and inappropriate teaching strategies.[20] This particular view of bilingual education was best summarized by Manuel Ramirez III when he said,

> We must view bilingual programs not only as providing opportunities for introducing the Spanish language, Mexican history, and Mexican American history into the system, but as vehicles for restructuring that system to insure the academic survival of Chicano children and the political and economic strength of the Chicano community.[21]

Fourth, many activists saw this reform as a means to deal more effectively with cultural assimilation. Initially, supporters looked at this program as a way to help minority children adjust to the Anglo culture of the school. But over the years, bilingual education was viewed as a means for preserving the Spanish language and Mexican culture of the Chicano and Chicana community. Bilingual education, noted Atilano A. Valencia, the director of Related Programs for Chicanos at the Southwestern Cooperative Educational Laboratory in Albuquerque, was "a quest for bilingual survival."[22]

These activists and countless others led the community's struggle against assimilationism and for both pluralism and academic success in the schools. By the end of the decade this effort was concentrated in the struggle for bilingual education in the United States.[23]

Impact of Context on Bilingual Education Proponents

These new social concerns coupled with research on bilingualism had significant implications for society in general and for the education of ethnic Mexican children in particular. They focused increased attention on the extent and effect of school discrimination on the ethnic identity and academic progress of poor Mexican-origin children.

With respect to the social implications, these studies added new dimensions to domestic issues of civil rights and poverty. More specifically, they extended the definition of discrimination to include language and culture. They also reinforced the notion that poverty had a linguistic dimension. These new studies likewise led to new attitudes towards bilingualism and bilinguals. Non-English languages came to be viewed in a positive light and as a precious resource that should be conserved. Bilinguals also came to be viewed more positively during these years. Finally, these studies seriously questioned the reality of the melting pot theory and provided support for cultural pluralism in American life.

These contextual forces also had educational implications. They led to a reassessment of specific educational practices that had detrimental impact on the ethnic identity and academic performance of poor Spanish speaking children. Among these practices were English-only laws, no-Spanish rules, and the structural exclusion of Mexican Americans from public education. Finally, they led to the promotion of language and culture-based school reforms such as the hiring of Spanish-speaking teachers, the incorporation of "non-English" languages and minority cultures into public education, and the repeal of English-only and no-Spanish speaking policies.

The early proponents of bilingual education took these novel ideas surrounding poverty and discrimination and applied them to the historic problems confronting schools with large numbers of Mexican children in the Southwest. In general they focused on explaining the historic pattern of underachievement experienced by Mexican-origin children and argued that they had negative school experiences, excessively high dropout rates, and low educational attainments because of poverty, negative attitudes towards Mexican-origin children and discriminatory school actions such as structural exclusion, school discrimination, cultural suppression, and inappropriate English-only instruction. Bilingualism, they added, would help reverse these historical patterns by replacing exclusionary, discriminatory and English-only school policies with native language instruction, a culturally appropriate curriculum, inclusive hiring practices, and strong parental involvement. Structural inclusion of community, language, and culture, in other words, would lead to increased school success among language minority children. It also would lead to minority political empowerment and to the replacement of assimilation ideals in this country with pluralism.

ENACTING FEDERAL BILINGUAL EDUCATION LEGISLATION, 1965–1968

The official push for bilingual education began with the publication of an important report issued by the National Education Association in 1966. This report publicized the negative impact of the schools on Mexican-American cultural identity and on their school performance. It documented many of the discriminatory educational policies affecting these children and argued that they contributed to low school performance and to alienation from the larger society. Traditional school policies and practices such as rigid "Anglicization" practices, English-only policies, no-Spanish speaking rules, and cultural degradation, the report argued, led to "damaged" self-esteem, resentment, psychological withdrawal from school and underachievement.[24]

This report not only documented the major problems confronting educators, it also proposed bilingualism as a solution for improving the education of Mexican-American children. Bilingualism, it argued, could help overcome decades of cultural degradation caused by rigid assimilationist policies and of exclusionary practices in the schools.[25] If schools hired Spanish-speaking teachers and adapted their curricular and administrative practices to the cultural and intellectual needs of Mexican-American children, it further argued, their self-esteem, cultural identity, and school performance would improve.[26]

The findings of this report served several important functions. First they presented a challenge to the dominant ideology of the causes of underachievement. According to existing views, poor school performance was due to the children's cultural background. Minority children such as Mexican Americans, the cultural deficit view stated, were not interested in education or did not desire it as strongly as other groups. The lack of motivation and desire thus accounted for their under-achievement.[27] The NEA report presented an alternative view. Discriminatory as well as traditional and non-accommodating school policies and practices, not the children's linguistic or cultural backgrounds, it argued, were responsible for underachievement.

Second, the NEA report challenged the dominant belief of assimilation, i.e., the idea that all individuals would eventually abandon their "foreign" languages and cultures and accept the idealized version of "American culture" as embodied in the Anglo-conformity or melting pot idea. English language learners such as Mexican Americans, it argued, were not melting and abandoning their linguistic and cultural heritage. This report also questioned whether assimilationism was an appropriate goal for the public schools. Bilingualism and cultural pluralism were more desirable goals than "melting pot-ism," it argued.

Unfortunately, the survey was unable to make a complete break with the dominant explanation of school performance. It still accepted the cultural deficit model as illustrated in the constant recognition of "handicaps" held by the Mexican-American children. Although it viewed the children's language as an asset for improving self-esteem and achievement, it continued to refer to it as a handicap. This implied that the school's role was to overcome this language handicap by helping them to learn English. English acquisition was to come at the expense of Spanish, or so this cultural deficit model implied. Despite these shortcomings, the NEA report represented a viable alternative to dealing with the problem of low achievement among Mexican Americans in the Southwest.

Finally, this report helped unify the diverse groups of educators and activists interested in improving the education of Mexican-American students. It also began the chain of events that eventually led to the enactment of the Bilingual Education Act of 1968.

NEA Planning Conference, 1966

Later that year, the NEA sponsored a planning conference to educate national, state, and local policymakers about the problems and solutions delineated in the 1966 survey findings and to encourage them to enact a federal bilingual education act that would serve the needs of Mexican-American schoolchildren. Under the guidance and leadership of Monroe Sweetland, conference organizers invited legislators, educators, researchers, and a variety of special interest groups, including Mexican-American activists. At the conference and through a variety of discussion sessions, participants were informed about the dimensions of the educational problems confronting schools with large numbers of Mexican-American students and the role that bilingual education could play in overcoming them. Policymakers were encouraged to enact such bills and the special interest groups were encouraged to build mass support for their enactment by hosting other state conferences.[28]

Formulation and Enactment of Bilingual Education, 1967

Several months after the Tucson conference, Ralph Yarborough, a U.S. Senator from Texas, introduced the first bilingual education act in the U.S. Two members of his staff, Alan Mandel and Gene Godley, worked with Monroe Sweetland, Guadalupe Anguiano, and Armando Rodriguez to draft this bill. Sweetland and Anguiano had worked on the NEA report and on the Tucson conference. Rodriguez was the first Mexican American appointed by President Lyndon Johnson to the U.S. Office of Education.[29] In order to appeal to other legislators outside of the Southwest, the bill was expanded to include all Spanish speakers in the U.S. During the negotiating process, legislators further expanded the definition of those to be served to include not only Spanish-speaking students but all non-English speaking students in the country.

In early January 1967, Senator Ralph Yarborough introduced the Bilingual American Education Act into the U. S. Senate. "Mr. President, the time for action is upon us," he said upon introducing this bill. Mexican Americans have not achieved equality of opportunity in this country, he noted, and they have been the victims of "the cruelest form of discrimination" in the schools. He further added

> English-only policies, no-Spanish speaking rules, and cultural degradation have caused great psychological harm to these children and contributed to their poor performance in school and high dropout rates. Bilingual education can overcome many of these problems and improve their academic achievement.[30]

Although many activities were suggested by this bill, the most important were those involving the use of the Spanish language. "Among Spanish-Americans," Yarborough stated, "the teaching of the Spanish language and culture to pupils who speak but do not read the language may provide a basis for motivation and an opportunity for achievement not previously accorded the group."[31]

During the next eleven months, support for bilingual education came from a variety of community organizations, civil rights groups and minority activists such as Mexican Americans. President Lyndon Baines Johnson, the Commissioner of Education, and a few politicians including Henry B. Gonzalez, Democratic congressperson from San Antonio, and John B. Connally, Democratic Governor of Texas, did not support the enactment of the bilingual education act. They were political enemies of Yarborough or else felt that the types of activities proposed by the bilingual bill could be developed under Title I of the Elementary and Secondary Education Act.[32]

External support for bilingual education came from the NEA, Mexican-American activists, and a few state departments of education. These groups or agencies, at the urging of the NEA or in cooperation with this organization, held a variety of conferences throughout the Southwest in support of finding solutions to the education of Mexican-American students. Four follow-up conferences were held in April 1967. Three of these were in California (Fresno, Bakersfield, and Los Angeles) and one in San Antonio, Texas. The final one was held in Pueblo, Colorado, in the fall of 1967. In all of these conferences, the participants passed strong resolutions in support of bilingual education legislation.[33]

Internal support for bilingual education was provided by legislators within the U.S. Congress. Key legislators held hearings in three states with significant numbers of Spanish-speaking children—Texas, California, and New York—and encouraged supporters to speak on behalf of this bill. Congressional allies also ensured that the bill passed both houses without serious modifications. In order to ward off potential opposition to the bill, the Senate Committee on Labor and Public Welfare adopted it as an amendment to the Elementary and Secondary Education Act of 1965. While this assured its passage in Congress, it also linked it up to poverty legislation and to its association with the War on Poverty.[34]

Individuals and groups supported this legislation for different reasons. Educators, as noted above, thought that this was the best instrument for improving achievement among these children. Bilingual education, especially the use of the child's native language, would help eliminate obstacles to achievement and promote cultural pride and self worth. Others felt that bilingual education could be an instrument of comprehensive educational change and reinforce home/school relations. Others still, especially the emerging Chicano movement advocates and language specialists, viewed bilingual education as an instrument of cultural and linguistic preservation.[35]

The Bilingual Education Act was enacted by Congress in December 1967 and signed into law one month later by President Lyndon Baines Johnson.[36]

In its final version, the bill targeted all children who were limited in their ability to speak English. The purpose of the Bilingual Education Act of 1968 was twofold:

(1.) to encourage the recognition of the special educational needs of limited English speaking children and

(2.) to provide financial assistance to local educational agencies to develop and carry out new and imaginative public school programs designed to meet these special educational needs.

The bill authorized a total of eighty-five million dollars for a three-year period. These funds could be used for a variety of purposes including planning, developing, and establishing "programs designed to meet the special educational needs of children of limited English-speaking ability in high poverty areas." Some funds could also be used to provide preservice and inservice training for teachers, miscellaneous professional staff, and paraprofessionals involved in these programs. The bill likewise mandated the Commissioner of Education to establish in the Office of Education an Advisory Committee on the Education of Bilingual Children to provide advice on the implementation of this policy.[37]

Responses to Bilingual Legislation

Minority spokespersons, legislators, and professional educators hailed the passage of this bill since it established a national policy recognizing the diverse language needs of minority children in education. At the same time, however, many of them realized that the act was a minor piece of legislation and an afterthought of the War on Poverty social legislation.[38] The Bilingual Education Act contained many weaknesses that needed to be corrected. There were at least five major problems with this bill.

First, the bilingual education bill was programmatically small in relation to existing poverty legislation. Only eighty-five million dollars were authorized for bilingual education but over one billion dollars for compensatory education programs. Despite its low authorization, the bilingual education bill received zero funding during the first year after its passage. Legislators began to authorize funds for this program only after its supporters lobbied the appropriate committees and agencies.[39]

Second, program participation was on a voluntary basis since there was no requirement for implementing bilingual education. Because there was no mandate, few school districts, as advocates found out later, took advantage of this bill during the first several years of its implementation. "Bilingual education," noted John C. Molina, the first Mexican-American director of the national Office of Bilingual Education, "was too new and philosophically threatening to be accepted by many school districts which often favored remedial and English language programs instead."[40]

Third, the program was categorical in nature and compensatory in intent. Categorical funds were provided by the federal government to local educational agencies to support services of a particular type or for a particular category of students. Under this new bill, funds were to be used to develop compensatory educational programs for those students who were limited in their ability to speak English and who came from low-income homes, i.e., those who were economically and "linguistically handicapped."

Fourth, it was "open-ended": it did not legally require or prescribe a particular curriculum nor insist on particular bilingual instructional techniques. Congress, in keeping with tradition, did not specify any one single approach to instructing English language learners. A variety of educational programs in addition to bilingual ones were eligible for funding under the new bill.[41]

Fifth, the programs' purpose was ambiguous, the definition of fundable programs was non-existent, and the goals were unspecified.[42] The lack of experienced teachers and of appropriate materials in non-English languages also created additional obstacles for the effective implementation of bilingual programs.[43]

CONCLUSION

The enactment of the federal Bilingual Education Act of 1968 culminated the initial phase of contemporary activism that originated in the beginning of the decade when language specialists, professional educators, non-white language minorities, and minority civil rights advocates began to agitate for improved educational opportunities for Mexican Americans. These groups, with their multiple perspectives and orientations, rejected the dominant assimilationist philosophies and discriminatory structures undergirding educational policy in this country. They also articulated oppositional ideologies and structures aimed at supporting pluralism, political empowerment, and significant educational change. More specifically, the motley crew of school activists took the key ideas advanced by the black and brown civil rights movement, the War on Poverty, and research on bilingualism and developed arguments in support of a particular form of bilingual education policy. This policy, many believed, would reverse the historic patterns of Mexican-American underachievement by acknowledging the role that non-English languages, cultures, and communities played in school success and by incorporating them into the structures and content of public education.

With these sets of beliefs and hopes, they fought against opposition within the federal government and against the passive resistance of many individuals and groups who misunderstood or were ignorant of the merits of native language instruction. In 1968, they succeeded in enacting the first federal bilingual education act. This bill, although important, was problematic and contained many weaknesses. It was programmatically small, categorical in nature, compensatory in intent, and voluntary. Also, the policy's purpose and the program's goals were undefined.

Although the bill was not exactly what they wanted, the proponents were not disillusioned. During the next decade or so, they took it upon themselves to change the character of this minor piece of legislation and to transform it into a major policy aimed at promoting bilingualism, cultural pluralism, and significant school change. The enactment of federal bilingual education legislation in 1968, in other words, initiated a new phase of ethnic and race relations in the history of American public schooling that soon polarized Americans along the lines of language, culture, ethnicity, and pedagogy.

NOTES

1. Diego Castellanos with Pamela Leggio-Castellanos, *The Best of Two Worlds: Bilingual-Bicultural Education in the U.S.* (Trenton, NJ: New Jersey State Department of Education, 1983); Mildred R. Donoghue, *Foreign Languages and the Elementary*

School Child (Dubuque, IA: William C. Brown Company Publishers, 1968); Gary D. Keller and Karen S. Van Hooft, "A Chronology of Bilingualism and Bilingual Education in the United States," in Joshua A. Fishman and Gary D. Keller, eds., *Bilingual Education for Hispanic Students in the U.S.* (NY: Teachers College Press, 1982), 3–19.

2. See Shirley Brice Heath, "Our Language Heritage: A Historical Perspective," June K. Phillips, ed., *The Language Connection: From the Classroom to the World* (Skokie, Ill.: National Textbook Company, 1977), 23–51; Maria Estela Briske, "Language Policies in American Education," *Journal of Education* 163: 1 (Winter 1981): 3–15; Arnold Leibowitz, *Educational Policy and Political Acceptance: The Imposition of English as the Language of Instruction in American Schools* (Wash.: ERIC, 1971); Heinz Kloss, *The American Bilingual Tradition* (Rowley, MA: Newbury House Publishers, Inc., 1977); and James Crawford, *Bilingual Education: History, Politics, Theory and Practice* (Trenton, NJ: Crane Publishing Company, Inc., 1989).

3. The terms used to describe the Mexican origin population in the U.S. are diverse and vary across time and space. For this reason, I will use the following terms interchangeably to make reference to this group: Mexican origin, ethnic Mexican, Mexican American and Chicano/Chicana. Occasionally, I will also use several broad terms indicative of groups whose national origins are from Spanish-speaking countries in Mexico, Central, and South America. Among the more common labels used in this study are Spanish-speaking, Latino, and Hispanic. The terms used for those children served by bilingual education programs likewise have varied over time and include the following: non-English speakers, limited-English speakers, limited-English proficient, and, more recently, English language learners.

4. Gaarder argues that bilingualism, despite problems, was not a matter of intelligence but of adequate teaching methods. See A. Bruce Gaarder, "Conserving Our Linguistic Resources," *PMLA* 80 (May 1965): 19–23.

5. Two important articles that helped to shift the emphasis of the impact of bilingualism on intelligence were Elizabeth Peal and Wallace Lambert, "The Relation of Bilingualism to Intelligence," *Psychological Monographs, General and Applied* 76 (1962): 1–23; and Joshua Fishman, "Bilingualism, Intelligence, and Language Learning," *Modern Language Journal* 49 (March 1965): 227–237.

6. Theodore Andersson, "A New Focus on the Bilingual Child," Paper presented at the Conference for the Teacher of the Bilingual Child, University of Texas, June 9, 1964 (In author's possession); A. Bruce Gaarder, "Teaching the Bilingual Child: Research,

Development, and Policy," Paper presented at the Conference for the Teacher of the Bilingual Child, University of Texas, June 10, 1964. (In author's possession.) See also Wallace E. Lambert and G. Richard Tucker, *Bilingual Education of Children: The St. Lambert Experiment* (Rowley, MA: Newbury House Publishers, Inc., 1972).

7. For a summary of research studies on bilingualism and language learning see A. Cohen, *A Sociolinguistic Approach to Bilingual Education* (Rowley, MA: Newbury House Publishers, Inc., 1976).

8. See, for instance, Joshua Fishman, "The Status and Prospects of Bilingualism in the U.S.," *Modern Language Journal* 49 (March 1965): 143–55; Chester C. Christian, Jr., "The Acculturation of the Bilingual Child," *Modern Language Journal* 69 (March, 1965): 160–65; and Joshua Fishman, *Language Loyalty in the United States* (The Hague: Mouton, 1966).

9. Fishman, *Language Loyalty*.

10. Nathan Glazer and Danial Moynihan, *Beyond the Melting Pot: The Negroes, Puerto Ricans, Jews, Italians, and Irish of New York City* (Cambridge, MA: M.I.T. Press, 1963).

11. For an overview of this period see the following sources: Harvard Sitkoff, *The Struggle for Black Equality, 1954–1992* (New York: Hill and Wang, 1993); Joel Spring, "Civil Rights," in *The Sorting Machine Revisited* (New York: Longman, 1989), 111–16; and Diane Ravitch, "Race and Education," in *The Troubled Crusade* (New York: Basic Books, Inc., 1983), 114–44. For a broader view of this period encompassing other groups besides blacks see Leonard Dinnerstein, Roger L. Nichols, and David M. Reimers, *Natives and Strangers: Blacks, Indians and Immigrants in America*, 2nd ed. (New York: Oxford University Press, 1990), 293–333.

12. Theodore Andersson, "A New Focus on the Bilingual Child," Paper presented at the Conference for the Teacher of the Bilingual child, University of Texas, June 9, 1964 (In author's possession); and Gaarder, "Teaching the Bilingual Child." For one of the earliest studies to document the impact of this type of discrimination on Mexican Americans in education, see Thomas P. Carter, *Mexican Americans in School* (New York: College Entrance Examination Board, 1970). See also Herschel T. Manuel, *Spanish-speaking Children of the Southwest* (Austin: University of Texas Press, 1965).

13. For a discussion of the importance of the War on Poverty and the role played by the Elementary and Secondary Education Act of 1965 see Spring, "War on Poverty," 111–16.

14. For examples of some of these studies see Joshua Fishman, "Childhood Indoctrination for Minority Group Membership," *Daedalus* 90:2 (Spring 1961): 329–49; and Mildred V. Boyer, "Poverty and the Mother Tongue," *Educational Forum* 29:3 (March 1965): 290–96.

15. Mildred V. Boyer, "Texas Squanders Non-English Resources," *Texas Foreign Language Association Bulletin* 5:3 (Oct 1963): 1–8; and Gaarder, "Conserving Our Linguistic Resources."

16. For an overview of their ideals, see Ignacio M. Garcia, *Chicanismo: The Forging of a Militant Ethos Among Mexican Americans* (Tucson: University of Arizona Press, 1997).

17. NEA, *The Invisible Minority* (Washington, D.C.: NEA, 1966); Armando Navarro, *The Cristal Experiment: A Chicano Struggle for Community Control* (Madison, WI: University of Wisconsin Press, 1998); Carlos Munoz, Jr., *Youth, Identity, Power: The Chicano Movement* (New York: Verso, 1990).

18. Manuel Ramirez III, "Bilingual Education as a Vehicle for Institutional Change," in Alfredo Castaneda et al., eds. *Mexican Americans and Educational Change* (New York: Arno Press, 1974), 387–407. See also Atilano A. Valencia, "Bilingual-Bicultural Education: A Quest for Institutional Reform," *Spring Bulletin* (Riverside, CA: Western Regional Desegregation Projects, University of California, Riverside, April 1971), 11.

19. During these years a few Mexican-American activists were distrustful of bilingual education and viewed it as an instrument of assimilation, not cultural pluralism. Luci Jaramillo, 1973, for instance, referred to bilingual education as a "por mientras" (in the meantime). See Mari-Luce Jaramillo, "The Future of Bilingual-Bicultural Education, in *Ghosts in the Barrio*, ed. Ralph Polana (San Rafael, CA: Leswing Press, 1973), 250–63. Her statement implied cautious support for this untried reform. Parents in Cristal City also voiced doubts about the development of a bilingual education program in that city in 1970. See John Staples Shockley, *Chicano Revolt in a Texas Town* (Notre Dame: University of Notre Dame Press, 1974), 163, 203. See also Carlos Munoz, Jr. *Youth, Identity, Power: The Chicano Movement.*

20. Carlos E. Cortés, "Revising the 'All-American Soul Course': A Bicultural Avenue to Educational Reform," in Alfredo Castaneda, et al, eds. *Mexican Americans and Educational Change* (New York: Arno Press, 1974), 314–39.

21. Manuel Ramirez III, "Bilingual Education as a Vehicle for Institutional Change," in Alfredo Castaneda, et al., eds. *Mexican Americans and Educational Change* (New York: Arno Press, 1974), 390–91. See more generally Guadalupe San Miguel, Jr., "Actors Not Victims: Chicanas/Chicanos and the Struggle for Educational Equality," in David R. Maciel and Isidro D. Ortiz, eds., *Chicanas/Chicanos at the Crossroads* (Tucson: University of Arizona Press, 1996), 159–80.

22. Atilano A. Valencia, "Bilingual Education: A Quest for Bilingual Survival," in Alfredo Castaneda, et al., eds., *Mexican Americans and Educational Change* (New York: Arno Press, 1974), 345–62. See as well Rubén Donato, *The Other Struggle for Equal Schools: Mexican Americans during the Civil Rights Era* (New York: SUNY Press, 1997); and Shockley, *Chicano Revolt.*

23. San Miguel, "Actors Not Victims."

24. NEA, *The Invisible Minority.*

25. The belief that preservation of the linguistic and cultural heritage of Mexican American and other language minority children could overcome cultural degradation and low school performance was quite common during this period. See, for instance, Gaarder, "Conserving Our Linguistic Resources"; Southwest Council of Foreign Language Teachers, "A Resolution Concerning the Education of Bilingual Children," in Theodore Andersson and Mildred Boyer, eds., *Bilingual Education in the United States* (Austin: Southwest Educational Development Laboratory, 1970), 284–86; Sister D.C. Noreen, "A Bilingual curriculum for Spanish-Americans: A Regional Problem with nation-wide Implications," *Catholic School Journal* 66:1 (Jan l966): 25–26; California Department of Education, *Bilingual Education for Mexican American Children* (Sacramento: Dept. of Education, l967); Francesco M. Cordasco, "The Challenge of the Non-English Speaking Child in American Schools," *School and Society* 96 (March 30, l968): 198–201.

26. NEA, *The Invisible Minority.*

27. For an overview of the dominance of cultural interpretations of low academic performance among Mexican Americans see Nick C. Vaca, "The Mexican-American in the Social Sciences, 1912–1970, Part I: 1912–1935," *El Grito* (Fall 1970): 3–16, 21–24; Nick C. Vaca, "The Mexican-American in the Social Sciences, 1912–1970, Part II: 1936–1970," *El Grito* (Fall 1971): 17–51; Thomas P. Carter, *Mexican Americans in Schools: A History of Educational Neglect* (New York: College Entrance Examination

Board, 1970; and Thomas P. Carter and R. D. Segura, *Mexican Americans in School: A Decade of Change* (New York: College Entrance Examination Board, 1979).

28. *Las Voces Nuevas del Sudoeste: A Symposium on the Spanish-speaking Child in the Schools of the Southwest, Tucson, Arizona, October 30–31, 1966* (Tucson, AZ: National Education Association, Committee on Civil and Human Rights of Educators of the Commission on Professional Rights and Responsibilities, 1966).

29. Gilbert Sanchez, "An Analysis of the Bilingual Education Act, 1967–1968" (Ph.D. diss., University of Massachusetts, 1973).

30. Ralph Yarborough, "Two Proposals for a Better Way of Life for Mexican Americans in the Southwest," *Congressional Record* (January 17, 1967): 599–600.

31. Yarborough, "Two Proposals," 600.

32. Sanchez, "An Analysis," 54–56.

33. For an overview of these conferences see Sanchez, "An Analysis," 52–58.

34. Sanchez, "An Analysis," 72–80.

35. For the variety of reasons given in support of bilingual education legislation see the following congressional hearings: U.S. Sen., *Bilingual Education, Hearings before the Special Subcommittee on Bilingual Education of the Committee on Labor and Public Welfare on S. 428* (2 vols.) 90th Cong., 1st Sess., 18–19, 26, 29, and 31 May 1967 (part 1), and 24 June and 21 July 1967 (Part 2), and House of Rep., *Bilingual Education Programs, Hearings before the General Subcommittee on Education of the Committee on Education and Labor on H.R. 9840 and H.R. 10224,* 90th Cong., 1st Sess., 28–29 June 1967.

36. *Bilingual Education Act of 1967,* Public Law 90–247, 81 Stat. 816, (1968).

37. *Bilingual Education Act of 1967;* for the authorization and uses of funds see Sec. 703 and Sec. 704, respectively. For the section on the establishment of the advisory committee see Sec. 707. Quotation appears on p. 816.

38. Colman Brez Stein, Jr., *Sink or Swim: The Politics of Bilingual Education* (Westport, CT: Praeger, 1986), 10–19.

39. Joshua Fishman, "The Politics of Bilingual Education," in Francesco Cordasco, ed., *Bilingual Schooling in the U.S.* (New York: McGraw-Hill Book Company, 1976), 141–49; Harman Badillo, "The Politics and Realities of Bilingual Education," *Foreign Language Annals* 5:3 (March 1972): 297–301.

40. See John C. Molina, "National Policy on Bilingual Education: An Historical View of the Federal Role," in Hernand LaFontaine, Barry Persky, and Leonard H. Golubchick, eds., *Bilingual Education* (Wayne, NJ: Avery Publishing Group, Inc., 1978), 17.

41. Stein, *Sink or Swim,* 10–19.

42. For a review of some of the major concerns in bilingual education during the 1970s see Hernand LaFontaine, Barry Persky, and Leonard H. Golubchick, eds., *Bilingual Education* (Wayne, NJ: Avery Publishing Group, Inc., 1978); Francesco Cordasco, ed., *Bilingual Schooling in the United States: A Sourcebook for Educational Personnel* (New York: McGraw Hill, 1976); and Stein, *Sink or Swim,* 10–19.

43. John C. Molina aptly stated the nature of the weaknesses and deficiencies of this bill at a national conference several years after its enactment. "The implementation of bilingual programs under the 1968 Bilingual Education Act, Title VII of the Elementary and Secondary Education Act," he stated, "revealed the weaknesses of the Act as well as the complexity of establishing programs with conflicting goals, untrained personnel, and inadequate instructional materials and evaluation." See John C. Molina, "National Policy on Bilingual Education: An Historical View of the Federal Role," in Hernand LaFontaine, Barry Persky, and Leonard H. Golubchick, eds., *Bilingual Education* (Wayne, NJ: Avery publishing Group, Inc., 1978), 16.

CHAPTER 2

THE EXPANSION OF BILINGUAL EDUCATION, 1968–1978

INTRODUCTION

During the first decade of its existence, from 1968 to 1978, bilingual education policy was strengthened and transformed as it was implemented. Federal court rulings, executive actions, and the political struggles of minority and non-minority group members contributed to its growth and strengthening.

The proponents of bilingual education constantly struggled for funds, created the administrative mechanisms for encouraging the establishment of bilingual education programs, provided definitions of and clashed over the goals and content of bilingual education, and developed a federal support system for its implementation. These developments led to a variety of programmatic, educational, and political changes and to the transformation in the goals, scope, and character of bilingual education. They also led to the emergence of an organized opposition to bilingual education policy.

TRANSFORMATION OF POLICY

Expand Scope of Legislation: From Categorical to Capacity Building

During the first decade of implementation, the scope of bilingual education legislation was expanded. This was reflected in the types of activities that the legislation funded and the amount of funding it received.

In 1968, the bilingual education act was categorical in nature. In keeping with federal legislative tradition, funding under the new bill was to be used by local educational agencies (LEAs) to develop innovative educational programs for specific categories of children, i.e., poor school children with limited English-speaking abilities. By the time it was reauthorized in 1974, the scope of bilingual education legislation had expanded to include more wide-ranging activities. In this year, the emphasis of legislation shifted from providing financial assistance for the development of innovative educational programs to improving the "capacity" of local school officials to provide bilingual education. This meant that bilingual education legislation would now provide funds for several types of activities. In addition to funding the development of educational programs, it would also provide funds for professional and teacher-training development, curriculum development, research and data collection, and federal administration of bilingual education.[1] With respect to the latter, for instance, the bill led to the establishment of a national office of bilingual education, a national advisory group of bilingual education, and a national clearinghouse on bilingual education.[2] These types of "capacity-building" activities were strengthened in 1978.[3]

The expanding scope of bilingual education legislation was also reflected in funding patterns. Funding for bilingual education, for instance, increased appreciably from $7.5 million to over $138 million between fiscal year 1969 and fiscal year 1978. (The fiscal year runs from October 1st to September 30th.)[4]

This increase in funds was a gradual and contested process. Although there was no overt opposition to the passage of this bill, the White House created obstacles. Under pressure from the White House, Congress failed to fund it during the fiscal year of its enactment.[5]

Despite White House claims to the contrary, Joshua Fishman argued that the major reason for no funding was due to lack of follow-up by the proponents of bilingual education. According to him, the proponents, new to national politics, had not realized that legislation was a never-ending process. Although Congress had authorized a new program, no

funds had been appropriated. In order to receive funds, the proponents
also had to lobby the appropriations committee. Instead, most of them
left Washington after the bill was enacted and none remained to lobby
for appropriations for this piece of legislation.[6]

Fishman not only criticized the proponents of bilingual education
for leaving town, he also called for the establishment of a bilingual education lobby and for closer ties with a variety of ethnic and educational
groups that might serve as allies for bilingual education.[7] His suggestions
were soon implemented in the struggle to strengthen this policy.

Pressures from different interest groups, especially Mexican-American
federal officials and community organizations, eventually led to the
funding of this bill. Between 1968 and 1969, for instance, funding for
bilingual education programs increased from zero level funding to $7.5
million. Four years later it increased to $75 million. By 1978, funding for
bilingual education was at $138 million.[8] Although funding levels were
still relatively small in contrast to those of Title I and other federal programs, they increased appreciably during the 1970s.

Modify Program: From Compensatory to Enrichment

The proponents of bilingual education also tried to change the compensatory character of this policy. They tried to turn it into an enrichment
program serving not only low income, limited-English-speaking children,
but all children regardless of language ability, ethnicity, or social class.

Bilingual education was enacted into law as part of the War on
Poverty programs. Poverty programs, in general, were based on the theory of cultural deprivation: the idea that the cultural values, languages,
and dialects spoken by minority children accounted for their poor
school performance. With respect to Mexican Americans, the Spanish
language and cultural values that they shared were viewed as deficits or
obstacles to learning. In order to succeed, these children had to abandon
them and acquire English. Compensatory programs such as bilingual
education were aimed at overcoming these types of deficits.[9]

Because it was viewed as a compensatory program by most legislators and educators, bilingual education targeted only those children who

were low-income and limited in their ability to speak English. "The Congress hereby finds that one of the most acute educational problems in the United States is that which involves millions of children of limited English-speaking ability because they come from environments where the dominant language is other than English," noted Congress in the first section of the bilingual education act. "[T]he urgent need," it further elaborated, "is for comprehensive and cooperative action now on the local, State, and Federal levels to develop forward-looking approaches to meet the serious learning difficulties faced by this substantial segment of the Nation's school-age population."[10]

Soon after its enactment, the advocates tried to eliminate the compensatory features of this policy so that all children in the United States, regardless of socioeconomic status or language ability, could enroll in these programs. Their first success came with the publication of the regulations for implementing bilingual education in 1969. In these guidelines, supporters of bilingual education deleted the poverty criteria for participation so that all limited-English-proficient (LEP) children could be eligible, not simply those who were low-income. They also developed a new regulation allowing English speakers to participate. "In an area eligible for a Title VII project," the regulations stated, "children from environments where the dominant language is English are eligible to participate when their participation is such as to enhance the effectiveness of the program."[11]

In 1974, the bilingual education bill incorporated the regulatory changes eliminating poverty as a requirement for participation in this program and allowing English speakers to enroll as well.[12] Four years later, the reauthorized bill set a limit on the percentage of English-speaking students eligible for participation in these programs. In this year, it stipulated that only up to forty percent of children in bilingual education could be English speakers.[13]

The 1974 and 1978 bilingual education bills also added Native American children as an eligible population. In earlier years, the emphasis had focused primarily on children who spoke European languages and had not made provisions for children who spoke Indian languages and dialects.[14]

These new provisions helped to transform bilingual education from a compensatory to an enrichment program. Whereas before only low-income, limited-English-proficient children were eligible for bilingual instruction, by 1978 English-speaking children as well as LEP children, regardless of socioeconomic status or language ability, could enroll in these types of programs.[15]

Despite these policy and regulatory changes, most educators, legislators, and lay persons continued to view bilingual education as a compensatory program and as part of the War on Poverty legislation. Much of this had to do with the attitude they had towards the targeted population. Most individuals still viewed language-minority children in deficit terms, as lacking in their ability to speak English. The failure to speak English, in turn, was viewed as an obstacle to academic performance. Although the label used to target these individuals gradually expanded and changed from limited-English speaking ability to limited-English-proficiency the idea of "deficiency" continued to permeate bilingual policy and practice.[16]

From Silence to Contestation (Goals)

Although Congress enacted a bilingual education bill in 1968, it did not specify what goals it hoped to accomplish. Congressional intent indicated that this policy would be aimed at improving the academic achievement of language minority children but policy did not specify how this would be done. By 1978, federal policy delineated certain goals but policymakers and supporters of bilingual education clashed over their meanings.

The 1968 bilingual bill acknowledged the existence of "serious learning difficulties" faced by children who were limited in their ability to speak English and who came from poverty backgrounds. It also provided funds to "develop forward-looking approaches" for resolving this issue. More specifically, it provided financial assistance to local school districts "to develop and carry out new and imaginative elementary and secondary school programs" designed to meet the special educational needs of these children.[17] No particular program, approach, or methodology was recommended. The bill stipulated that among the approved activities were: bilingual education, teaching the history and culture of the targeted population, improving school-community relations, early childhood education, adult education, vocational education, drop-out programs, or "other activities which meet the purposes of this title."[18] Although bilingual education was mentioned as an approved activity, the legislation did not define what this was nor did it specify the role of native language instruction in this program.

During the next several years, scholars, policymakers, and educators decried, among other things, the lack of goal stipulation in this policy.[19] A public debate about goals quickly emerged in the early 1970s. This public debate, however, narrowly defined the issue as one of language learning and cultural development rather than academic achievement. The major questions framing the debate became: should bilingual education promote English fluency or bilingualism and should it promote assimilation or pluralism?[20] These discussions occurred in the context of official White House opposition to this program and passive resistance to pluralism among legislators.[21]

In 1974, legislators clarified the goal of federal policy and provided a definition of bilingual education. The goal of bilingual education was embedded in its definition. The policy goal became one of providing equal educational opportunity for all children through the establishment and operation of bilingual education programs. Few, if any, individuals or organizations raised concerns about this policy goal. Most, if not all, actors involved in policy formation were in agreement with this broad goal. Disagreements, misinterpretations, and conflicts, however, emerged over the goals implied in the definition of bilingual education.

The reauthorized bill defined bilingual education as "instruction given in, and study of, English and, to the extent necessary to allow a child to progress effectively through the educational system, the native language of the children of limited English-speaking ability. . . ." Additionally, it stipulated that "such instruction is given with appreciation for the cultural heritage of such children. . . ."[22]

The 1974 Bilingual Education Act complicated matters by encouraging multicultural understanding among English-speaking children. A new provision in this bill allowed English-speaking children to enroll in this program in order "that they may acquire an understanding of the cultural heritage of the children of limited English speaking ability for whom the particular program of bilingual education is designed."[23] This provision appeared to be aimed at eliminating the compensatory character of bilingual education by encouraging the participation of all children, not merely those who lacked English fluency, in bilingual programs. Regardless of the reason for its inclusion, it added to the notion that bilingual education policy had become an instrument for the promotion of bilingualism and cultural pluralism.

The inclusion of native language instruction and cultural appreciation in the definition of bilingual education led to the origins of a contentious public debate over the goals of this policy. Should bilingual education use the children's native language only until they could speak English or should it maintain their native language even after they learned English? The former model was called transitional bilingual education, the latter maintenance bilingual education.[24] Also, should the schools promote assimilation or the preservation of ethnic minority cultures?

Most proponents of this policy interpreted this definition to mean that bilingual education had two major goals: the promotion of bilingualism and of cultural pluralism. For years, language specialists, educators, Latino/Latina activists, and others had supported using federal legislation to preserve the distinct languages and cultures of ethnic minority groups.[25] Their inclusion in the 1974 bill suggested that they had succeeded in reaching this objective.[26] The children enrolled in this program now would learn English and maintain their native language, they argued. They also would receive instruction in their "native" culture as they learned English.

Political leaders within the Office of Education vehemently disagreed with this interpretation and argued that bilingual education legislation was consistently clear: the purpose of bilingual education during the 1970s was "to achieve competence in the English language."[27] Although the bill allowed for the use of the native language and of the "native" culture, they were merely means to an end, not ends in themselves. The Under Secretary for Education, Frank Carlucci, best stated the Department of Health, Education and Welfare's position on bilingual education in early December 1974. He stated:

> A frequent misunderstanding, which seems to have provoked unnecessary and fruitless debate over bilingual policy is the failure to distinguish the goals of bilingual/bicultural programs from the means of achieving them. P.L 93–380 (the Bilingual Education Act of 1974) emphasizes strongly that "a primary *means* by which a child learns is through the use of such child's language and cultural heritage . . . and that children of limited English-speaking ability benefit through the fullest utilization of multiple language and cultural resources." But the law makes it equally clear that the ultimate goal of Federal bilingual education programs is "to demonstrate effective ways of providing for children of limited English-speaking ability, instruction designed to enable them, while using their native language, *to achieve competence in the English language.*"[28]

Carlucci's comments in many ways were more accurate than the interpretations offered by the proponents of bilingual education. Although the bilingual bill acknowledged the role that the native language could play while targeted children learned English, it did not promote bilingual education as an enrichment program where the native language was maintained.[29] Neither did it help to preserve the minority cultures. The reasons for their use were not to preserve or maintain these languages and culture but to allow limited-English-speaking children to progress effectively through the educational system while they learned English. The primary goal of bilingual education, in other words, was English fluency.

The primacy of English learning, in fact, continued to be reflected in policy and program development for the next several years. In 1978, greater emphasis was placed on the goal of English learning in the new bilingual education bill. Unlike four years earlier when Congress encouraged the use of native languages in order to allow a child to progress through the educational system, in 1978 it stipulated that the reason for its use was "to allow a child to achieve competence in the English language. . . ." Congress also reaffirmed the importance of English learning as a goal in its reference to the participation of English speakers in bilingual education programs. According to the new bill the objective of their participation was "to assist children of limited English proficiency to improve their English language skills."[30]

Research and evaluation studies, likewise, indicated that the vast majority of bilingual programs during the 1970s were aimed at discouraging the maintenance of native languages and at facilitating language shift among minority children.[31]

From Voluntary to Mandatory

The proponents of bilingual education also strengthened this program through the courts, federal agencies, and the legislature. Initially, bilingual program participation was voluntary. In the enactment of this bill, Congress continued the principle of local control by allowing local school districts the option of participating in this federal program.

In the first several years of this policy, however, only a small proportion of school districts with large numbers of limited-English-speaking individuals applied for federal bilingual education funds. The indifference and unwillingness of local school officials to participate in bilingual education efforts led to political demands from a host of special interest and minority groups for its further strengthening. It also led to the filing of several lawsuits to pressure local school districts to apply for federal funds and to establish bilingual education programs for these children.[32]

By 1978, the option to participate had disappeared. All local educational agencies had to establish a bilingual education program if they had significant numbers of English-language learners. Failure to establish bilingual education would lead to a lawsuit or to a withdrawal of all federal school funds.

Civil rights policies became instrumental in the trend away from voluntary to mandatory policies and towards a federal preference for bilingual education approaches. In certain respects, then, bilingual education involved more than meeting the educational needs of English language learners; it also became a tool for ensuring their civil rights, i.e., for ensuring that language minority group children were not discriminated against on the basis of their language or cultural heritage.

Three specific policies and actions—the *Lau v. Nichols* decision of 1974, the *Lau* Remedies of 1975, and the *Lau* compliance reviews—added a mandatory aspect to federal bilingual education policy.[33] These policies mandated the participation of all school districts with significant numbers of language minority group children in bilingual education program development. They also narrowed the choices available to local school districts by discounting the use of English as a Second Language (ESL) methods and by mandating only methods that utilized the child's native languages and cultures.

Lau *Decision, 1974*

The *Lau v. Nichols* decision was the result of a school district in San Francisco that did not take advantage of the bilingual bill in order to establish programs that would improve the schooling of non-English-speaking children in its school district. The court ruled that it was unconstitutional to deny non-English speaking children, in this case Chinese students, instructional services in a language that they understood. It also ruled that local school districts had to take affirmative steps to rectify the language "deficiency" experienced by these children in order to open its instructional program to these students. Although many proponents argued that the *Lau* decision mandated bilingual education, it did not. The decision, however, did increase the local school's responsibility in ensuring that non-English speaking children received an appropriate instruction in the schools.[34]

The decision was based not on the constitutional denial of equal protection, but on the statutory and regulatory decisions pertaining to equal educational opportunity. More specifically, it reaffirmed the importance of the May 25th Memo drafted by the OCR in 1970.[35] Prior to this year, all existing anti-discrimination laws applied to African Americans. None made reference to children who were culturally and linguistically

different. To remedy the absence of Mexican Americans in federal programs, the federal government, in 1970, developed a wide-ranging policy
known as the May 25th Memo that stipulated the responsibilities of local
school districts to English language learners. In general, it stipulated that
discrimination on the basis of national origin in general and language in
particular was prohibited in any agency receiving federal funds.[36]

Lau *Remedies, 1975*

The *Lau* decision created much confusion in the schools since many
school districts did not know how to interpret it. In an effort to provide
guidance, the Office for Civil Rights, in 1975, issued a document specifying the remedies available to school districts for eliminating those educational practices ruled unlawful under the *Lau* decision.

The *Lau* Remedies, as it came to be known, unfortunately created
more problems for school officials and increased their opposition to
bilingual education as well as to the federal government's involvement
in it. More specifically, it discredited English language approaches to
educating language minority children and declared that bilingualism
was the only appropriate approach for improving educational access to
the curriculum and school performance. An English as a Second Language (ESL) program, noted the Lau Remedies, was not an appropriate
approach for elementary school children because it did not "consider
the affective nor cognitive development of students in this category and
time and maturation variables are different here than for students at the
secondary level." Acceptable programs for complying with the *Lau* decision of 1974 included any one or a combination of the following programs: transitional, bilingual/bicultural, and multilingual/multicultural
program. None of these programs were clarified but they all stipulated
the use of non-English languages and cultures in instruction.[37] This
document, in summary, established a federal preference for bilingual
education.

Lau *Remedies Compliance Reviews, 1975–78*

In addition to these procedures, the federal government also developed an elaborate civil rights enforcement mechanism and pressured local school districts to develop bilingual education programs. Although there were programmatic and interpretational problems and even opposition to the *Lau* Remedies, the Office for Civil Rights used it to negotiate compliance plans with over 500 local school districts in the late 1970s. Coercion or the threat of coercion and the withdrawal of federal school funds served as the basis for the development of bilingual education programs.[38]

IMPACT OF FEDERAL BILINGUAL EDUCATION POLICY

The origins of and changes in federal bilingual education policy had a significant impact on various aspects of American political and educational life. For instance, this policy significantly impacted state and local governments, the political fortunes of minority groups, and language use. More importantly, it encouraged a political opposition to voice its opinion and to speak out against this policy.

Language Use

Bilingual education encouraged what some opponents later called "creeping" bilingualism into American public life. Bilingualism in national public life expanded and grew as provisions allowing the use of non-English languages were rapidly added to other pieces of Congressional legislation such as the Emergency School Assistance, Vocational and Adult Education, Library Services, Indian Education, Cooperative Research, Higher Education, and Educational Professional Development Acts.[39]

Bilingual provisions were also added to areas outside of education during this period. For example, in 1975, an amendment to the Voting Rights Act provided for bilingual voting and registration materials when any minority exceeded five percent of the relevant electoral district.[40]

The enactment of the federal bilingual education act encouraged several states to eliminate their English-only laws and to enact their own bilingual bills. Between 1968 and 1974, sixteen states enacted some form of bilingual bills.[41] During the next four years, over thirty-four states enacted bilingual education legislation. According to Crawford, nine of these states required bilingual education under certain circumstances, twenty-one provided some form of financial aid to bilingual programs, and most set standards for certifying bilingual or ESL teachers.[42]

The five states of the Southwest, which contained a majority of the ethnic Mexican population, also enacted bilingual education legislation. California, in response to the NEA report and to the educational conferences of 1966, enacted legislation in 1967 permitting the use of non-English languages in the public schools. In 1969, the New Mexico state legislature adopted a law permitting any school district to set up "a bilingual and bicultural program of study." The state of Arizona enacted a law in 1969 permitting the establishment of special programs of bilingual instruction in the first three grades of all the public schools. Texas enacted a bilingual education bill in 1971.[43]

Bilingual education bills at the state level were originally permissive, similar to the federal act. That is, they permitted local school districts to establish special educational programs or services that utilized Spanish or other non-English languages as a medium of instruction. Over the years, these bills were gradually strengthened and their provisions expanded. In the early 1970s, both the New Mexico and Arizona state legislatures strengthened their legislation by making many of the bilingual education provisions mandatory.[44] California strengthened its bilingual bill in 1973 with the passage of the Bilingual Multi-Cultural Education Act. It provided for bilingual teaching in Kindergarten through sixth grade. Three years later, the bill was further strengthened and its provisions expanded. Unlike prior years, under this new bill most local school districts were mandated to provide bilingual education programs and services if they each had a certain number of language-minority children attending the schools. Texas strengthened its bilingual act in 1975 by adding certain mandatory provisions. If a school had more than twenty-five LEP children per grade level, it had to establish a bilingual class and hire a bilingual teacher.[45]

The rapid growth of institutional bilingualism was not only limited to the federal and state governments. It also grew in private life as many companies and corporations incorporated Spanish and other languages into their business practices. McDonald's, for instance, developed bilingual menus, especially along the U.S. border. Beer companies began to publicize their ads in Spanish on TV, magazines, and in community events.[46]

Bilingualism was truly increasing and transforming American life. Federal bilingual education policy both reflected and encouraged this trend.

Political Empowerment

The enactment and implementation of bilingual education in American schools led to the increased political empowerment of historically excluded minority groups such as Mexican Americans. Federal bilingual education programs, in other words, increased minority political involvement in education. For instance, it encouraged existing Mexican-American organizations such as the LULAC (League of United Latin-American Citizens), the Mexican American Political Association, the Political Association of Spanish-Speaking Organizations, the American G. I. Forum, and others to become actively involved in the enactment and implementation of bilingual education policies.[47]

Bilingual education also encouraged the establishment of new professionally oriented organizations. The National Association for Bilingual Education (NABE) became one of the most important and influential organizations of the 1970s. A variety of statewide organizations such as the California Association for Bilingual Education and the Texas Association for Bilingual Education assumed important roles in the promotion of bilingual education policies and programs in the U.S. and in the establishment, administration, and operation of bilingual education programs.

Ethnic Mexican and Latino parent groups also increased their involvement in school issues. Although parent groups were relatively ineffective in school policy, they aggressively sought ways to impact the establishment and implementation of bilingual programs in the schools.[48]

Finally, Mexican American and other Latino educators and scholars became actively involved in conducting, publishing, and disseminating bilingual education research projects and studies.[49]

The community, long excluded from the structures of power, now became actively involved in bilingual educational matters and in the promotion of their academic, linguistic, and cultural interests in the schools.

The Federal Role

Finally, the establishment of bilingual education policy led to the increased involvement of the federal government in local education. Initially, the federal role in the late 1960s was limited to congressional funding of a variety of educational activities at the local level. By the late 1970s all three branches of the federal government and most branches of the state and local governments were involved in the establishment and operation of bilingual education.

In 1968, the U. S. Congress was the only federal agency involved in bilingual education. Soon after the bill's enactment, a few agencies in the executive branch of the federal government became involved in a variety of ways, including the Department of Education (DOE), the Office of Bilingual Education, and the Office for Civil Rights (OCR). For instance, in 1969 the DOE was given the responsibility of developing regulations for the implementation of bilingual education legislation. Its involvement increased in the mid-1970s after the Comptroller General of the U.S. reported that it failed to provide strong leadership and to adequately manage program development. More specifically, this office failed to identify effective instructional approaches for national dissemination, to determine the extent of teacher shortages related to staffing of bilingual education programs, and to develop suitable curricular materials for them.[50]

In the mid-1970s, other offices within the Department of Education became involved in various aspects of bilingual education, especially in the oversight of this program. For instance, the DOE established a national bilingual education office to screen, monitor, and implement bilingual program policies, programs, and practices, hired a national director of bilingual education, established an Advisory Council on Bilingual Education, and vigorously monitored the development of regulations for the implementation of bilingual education policies. The OCR in the Department of Education became increasingly active in activities related to the compliance of the *Lau* decision.

The federal judiciary also became involved in bilingual education during the mid-1970s. The Supreme Court, as noted earlier, made a ruling favorable to bilingual education in 1974. Soon thereafter, several lower courts ruled on behalf of bilingual education advocates by mandating the use of native languages in the instruction of limited-English-proficient children and by prohibiting the use of ESL methods.[51]

By the latter part of the 1970s, then, the federal role had increased tremendously as indicated by the participation of all three branches of the federal government in the making, implementing, and evaluating of bilingual education policy. It had also become more actively involved in local education by mandating bilingual education throughout the country.

THE EMERGING OPPOSITION

Developments in federal bilingual education also impacted the political opposition and encouraged a few daring individuals to speak out against this policy. This initial opposition to bilingual education was reflected in two major studies that appeared in the late 1970s. These documents raised a whole series of questions about the goals, consequences, and effects of federal bilingual education.

The first study critical of federal bilingual education policy was published in 1977. In this year, Noel Epstein, a well-known conservative Washington journalist, raised fundamental questions about this piece of legislation.

One question he raised concerned bilingual education's effectiveness. Epstein argued that the original Bilingual Education Act of 1968 was a small, exploratory measure aimed at poor children who were "educationally disadvantaged" because of their inability to speak English. While allowing for a multitude of special educational programs for limited-English-speaking students, the federal government had come to recognize transitional bilingual education as the most appropriate method for these children. But "after nearly nine years and more than half a billion dollars in federal funds," he concluded, "the government has not demonstrated whether such instruction makes much difference in the students' achievement, in their acquisition of English, or in their attitudes towards school."[52]

Another question he raised related to the targeted population: the children. According to him, the definitions of eligible children in federal policies were broad enough to include many pupils who were actually proficient in English, although they also spoke another language. Since resources were limited and children who could not learn effectively in English were numerous, the federal government had to make a choice between using these resources to assist those most in need or to help fund programs aimed at providing instruction to students who were already proficient in English.[53]

The final and most important issue he raised concerned the role that the federal government should play in promoting education. He argued that the proponents of bilingual education sought a policy of "affirmative ethnicity." By this he meant that they sought sponsorship of language maintenance efforts while limited English children went through the normal process of learning the common English language and the common national history. Although the philosophy of affirmative ethnicity raised serious social questions concerning the assimilation of cultural groups into American society and the further segregation of language minority children in the public schools, another more fundamental issue was involved, he noted.

> The issue—and this cannot be emphasized too strongly—is not the unquestioned importance of ethnicity in individuals' lives, any more than it is the unquestioned importance of religion in individuals' lives. The issue is not the right or the desirability of groups to maintain their languages and cultures. The issue is the government role. The overriding question is whether the federal government is responsible for financing and promoting student attachments to

their ethnic languages and cultures, jobs long left to families, religious groups, ethnic organizations, private schools, ethnic publications, and others.[54]

The federal government, he argued, had no business in promoting minority languages and cultures. Its role now needed to be cut back.

The proponents of bilingual education responded vehemently to this report. One of the most thorough responses was by Jose A. Cardenas. He took issue with many of Epstein's argument and systematically challenged them.[55] "It is almost impossible to critique the many erroneous or opinionated statements found in Mr. Epstein's study," he noted. "Efforts to group them invariably lead to an excess of classifications, making the critique extremely long, repetitious and shallow," he added. Nonetheless, he meticulously critiqued three consecutive pages of the study and showed the many discrepancies and inaccuracies in it. With respect to Epstein's notion that the federal government promoted "affirmative ethnicity, with all forms of innuendos about separatism, un-Americanism and minority power" Cardenas argued:

> The federal government does not finance or promote pupil attachments to our ethnicity—these attachments we formed at our mother's breasts. The federal government finances and promotes understanding, respect and acceptance of other cultures; that is, other heritages, other traditions, values and orientation, and other lifestyles.[56]

Cardenas acknowledged the existence of problems in bilingual education but argued that they were primarily administrative ones. He concluded that "bilingual and bicultural education are not only pedagogically sound concepts, but are a positive step in bringing about equality of opportunity and the realization of the American dream for populations being excluded from the political, social, economic and educational mainstream."[57]

The second major study critical of bilingual education appeared in 1978 and was issued by a group of professional evaluators opposed to bilingual education. Known as the "AIR Report," it was named after the group conducting the research: the American Institutes for Research. This national evaluation reported that bilingual education did not appear to be having a consistent significant impact on student achievement in English language arts, math, or English reading, and in some cases, was having a negative result on LEP children. Bilingual education, in other words, was not an effective program.[58]

This report, I might add, was the culmination of several years of efforts by proponents to encourage the evaluation of bilingual education programs. Because of its recent development, few studies were available on the effectiveness of bilingual education during the latter part of the 1960s and early 1970s. During these important years, educators and scholars complained about the lack of evaluation in bilingual education program implementation and pleaded for collecting evaluative information on them to see if they were working.[59]

Some studies began to emerge in the mid-1970s but they were not favorable. Most of the authors of these reports, however, were supportive of bilingual education and tended to blame a host of factors including inadequate resources, inadequate placement, failure to use the native language in instruction, and inadequate monitoring by the Department of Education.

The first two studies evaluating bilingual education appeared in 1972. These studies, conducted by the federal government, showed mixed results. The first one was commissioned by Edward Kennedy in July 1972. As part of its study the General Accounting Office (GAO) conducted a six-month evaluation of twenty-eight bilingual education projects. Its major finding was that "the vast majority of the children's classroom time was spent sitting in classes where subjects were taught in English."[60] The second report was part of a comprehensive study of Mexican-American education in the Southwest. It described the exclusionary practices of schools in dealing with the unique linguistic and cultural characteristics of Chicano students. Its major findings were that the language and culture of Chicano children were ignored and even suppressed by the school. The school curriculum rarely included programs and courses designed to meet the particular needs of these students. In addition, Mexican-American parents were largely excluded from participation in school affairs.[61]

Another evaluation was conducted in 1973. In this year, the Comptroller General evaluated sixteen projects throughout the country. The results, based on both one-year and longitudinal data, indicated that LEP children made fewer gains than English-speaking children in reading and math. The program did positively affect the non-cognitive areas of self-image, cultural understanding, and attendance, but since no objective data was provided they were not seriously considered.[62] Three possible factors, it argued, might have adversely affected the academic achievement of LEP children in these programs. First, the dominant language of LEP children might not have been used enough in instruction. Second, too many English-speaking children in the program who diluted services for these children might have been present. Third, assessing English language proficiencies of the target population for placement purposes was too difficult. It also suggested that the Office of Education's monitoring of the program's implementation was inadequate.[63]

Because of the many problems these reports faced, the federal government set out to conduct a comprehensive national evaluation of bilingual education. The evaluation of bilingual education, however, became involved in national politics over the election of the president of the U.S. The report issued in 1978 thus was tainted to begin with since it became part of a Republican plan to undermine an educational policy developed and supported by Democrats.

The AIR Report, as noted above, indicated that bilingual education did not appear to be having a consistently significant impact on student achievement in English language arts, math, or English reading, and in some cases, was having a negative result on LEP children. The proponents of bilingual education quickly wrote critical responses to this report. They argued that it was politically-inspired and flawed in its research design and methodology. Jose Cardenas, for instance, argued that there were major discrepancies in the identity of the target group, the selection of comparable control groups, the test instruments used, the amount of time between pre-and post-testing, the programs being studied, the adequacy of instructional staff, and the sources of funds being used.[64] A particularly biting critique was issued by Robert A. Cervantes, an educator from California. Cervantes' critique, unlike most of his contemporaries', was broad in scope and went beyond criticizing technical aspects of the evaluation. He provided an overview of the events leading to the awarding of the contract to conduct a national evaluation of bilingual education and explained the reasons for acceptance of a "flawed" proposal. He argued that the award to AIR was related to the politics of Watergate (Nixon's reelection committee) and was part of a systematic plan to deprive Development Associates—the alternative group of evaluators—of federal contracts.[65]

Despite these criticisms, the AIR Report raised serious questions about the effectiveness of bilingual education. It was the first report to do so.

CONCLUSION

The passage of the Bilingual Education Act of 1968 was viewed in extremely positive terms by legislators, educators, and activists of all sorts. Despite its enactment, bilingual education was a minor, compensatory, and voluntary piece of legislation. During the next decade the proponents of bilingual education began to change its character and to transform the policy as it was being implemented. They expanded the scope of bilingual education legislation, contested the goals of this program, increased its funding, eliminated its compensatory provisions, and made it mandatory. In doing so, they significantly increased the federal role in local education.

The expansion of bilingual education policy also accompanied and contributed to the increased use of non-English languages in American institutional life and empowered minority individuals without significantly improving the scholastic achievement of LEP children.

Despite the growth of bilingual education policies during the 1970s, they tended to be assimilationist or "subtractive" in nature. That is, they accelerated and facilitated the learning of English among language minority children at the expense of the first language. Their subtractive nature, however, was overlooked by many individuals who viewed the growth of non-English language usage in public life as a threat to the political stability and cultural uniformity of this country.

The changed character of bilingual education policy, the increased presence of non-English languages and cultures, and the structural inclusion of ethnic minorities created fears and anxieties among Americans of all colors and raised significant issues about the country's national identity, minority political empowerment, effective pedagogy, and federalism, i.e., the nature of relations between the federal government and the states. These developments, especially the mandatory and non-English language aspects of bilingual education policy, sparked a vigorous opposition among local school officials, parents, and lay persons. The emerging opposition to bilingual education initially was diffused but it gathered steam in the 1980s. The following chapters document the impetus for its emergence and the impact it had on bilingual education policy.

NOTES

1. The capacity building emphasis of the bill was reflected in the different parts of the bill. Part A focused on financial assistance for bilingual education programs. Part B emphasized administrative aspects, and Part C focused on supportive services and activities such as research and demonstration projects as well as data collection on the size and nature of the non-English speaking student population. *Public Law 93–380,* Aug. 21, 1974, Parts A, B, C.

2. *PL 93–380,* Aug. 21, 1974, Parts A, B, C.

3. See *Public Law 95–562,* 1978, Parts A, B, C, and D.

4. Comptroller General Office, *Bilingual Education: An Unmet Need* (Washington, D.C.: GPO, May 19, 1976); *The Condition of Bilingual Education in the Nation-First Report by the U.S. Commissioner of Education to the Congress and the President* (Fall River, MA: National Assessment and Dissemination Center, November, 1976); *Strengthening Bilingual Education: A Report from the Commissioner of Education to the Congress and the President* (Washington, D.C.: United States Office of Education, Dept. of Health, Education, and Welfare, June 1979).

48CONTESTED POLICY

5. James Crawford, *Bilingual Education: History, Politics, Theory* (Trenton: Crane Publishers, 1989), 33.

6. Joshua Fishman, "The Politics of Bilingual Education," in Francesco Cordasco, ed., *Bilingual Schooling in the U.S.* (New York: McGraw-Hill Book Company, 1976), 141–49. For a similar analysis see Herman Badillo, "The Politics and Realities of Bilingual Education," *Foreign Language Annals* 5:3 (March 1972): 297–301.

7. Fishman, "The Politics of Bilingual Education," 141–49. For a similar analysis see Badillo, "The Politics and Realities."

8. Comptroller General Office, *Bilingual Education: An Unmet Need* (Washington, D.C.: GPO, May 19, 1976); *The Condition of Bilingual Education in the Nation-First Report by the U.S. Commissioner of Education to the Congress and the President* (Fall River, MA: National Assessment and Dissemination Center, November, 1976).

9. Richard R. Valencia, ed., *The Evolution of Deficit Thinking: Educational Thought and Practice* (Washington, D.C.: Falmer Press, 1997).

10. *PL 90–247,* January 2, 1968, 81 Stat. 817, Sec. 701.

11. The regulations issued in 1969 stated: "Children with limited English-speaking ability are eligible to participate (in bilingual programs) even though they are not from families with incomes below $3,000 per year, or from families receiving payments under a program of aid to families with dependent children under a State plan approved under Title IV of the Social Security Act." See the draft guidelines to the Bilingual Education program found in "Financial Assistance for Bilingual Education Programs," *Federal Register* 34, no.4 (Tuesday, 7 Jan. 1969): 201–5.

12. *Public Law 93–380,* Aug. 21, 1974, Sec 702(a.) and Sec. 703 (a)(4)(B).

13. *Public Law 95–561,* Nov. 1, 1978, Sec. 703 (a)(4)(A). The section stipulating the percent of English speakers in the program is found in *Public Law 95–561,* Nov. 1, 1978, Sec. 703 (a)(4)(B).

14. *Public Law 93–380,* Aug. 21, 1974, Sec. 722 (a)(5.); *Public Law 95–561,* Nov. 1, 1978, Sec. 722 (a).

15. The children's language, however, was still viewed as "deficient" by most educators. See Valencia, *The Evolution.*

16. The label used for the targeted population was changed to "limited English proficiency" in 1978. See *Public Law 95–561,* Nov. 1, 1978, 92 Stat. 2269, Sec. 703(a)(1).

17. *Public Law 90–247,* January 2, 1968, 81 Stat. 817, Sec. 702.

18. *Public Law 90–247,* January 2, 1968, 81 Stat. 817, Sec. 704, (c.) [1–8].

19. Garland Cannon, "Bilingual Problems and Developments in the United States," *PMLA* 86 (May 1971): 452–58; Theodore Andersson, "Bilingual Education: The American Experience," *Modern Language Journal* 55 (Nov. 1971): 427–40; Maria M. Swanson, "Bilingual Education: The National Perspective," in Gilbert A. Jarvis, ed., *The ACTFL Review of Foreign Language Education,* Vol. 5 (Skokie, IL: National Textbook, 1974), 75–127; Lawrence Wright, "Bilingual Education Movement at the Crossroads," in Earl J. Ogletree and David Garcia, eds., *Education of the Spanish speaking Child* (Springfield, IL.: Charles C. Thomas, 1975), 335–45.

20. A. Bruce Gaarder, "Bilingual Education: Central Questions and Concerns," in Hernan LaFontaine, ed., *Bilingual Education* (Wayne, NJ: Avery Publishing Group, Inc., 1978), 33–38; Robert F. Roeming, "Bilingualism and the National Interest," in Hernan LaFontaine, ed., *Bilingual Education* (Wayne, NJ: Avery Publishing Group, Inc., 1978), 78–81.

21. James A. Banks, *Multiethnic Education,* 2nd ed. (Boston: Allyn & Bacon, 1988), 3–18.

22. *Public Law 93–380,* Aug. 21, 1974, Sec 702 (a)(5).

23. *Public Law 93–380,* Aug. 21, 1974, Sec. 703 (a)(4)(B).

24. George Blanco, "The Education Perspective," in *Bilingual Education: Current Perspectives,* Vol. 4 (Arlington, VA: Center for Applied Linguistics, 1977), 21–52.

25. See, for instance, Francesco Cordasco, "The Challenge of the Non-English Speaking Child in American Schools," *School and Society* 106 (March 30 1968): 198–201; Joshua Fishman, *Language Loyalty in the United States: The Maintenance and Perpetuation of Non-English Mother Tongues by American Ethnic And Religious Groups* (The Hague: Mouton, 1966); A. Bruce Gaarder, "Conserving Our Linguistic Resources," *PMLA* 80 (May 1965): 19–23. Enrique T. Trueba, "Issues and Problems in Bilingual Bicultural Education Today," *Journal of the National Association for Bilingual Education* 1 (December 1976): 11–19; Lourdes Travieso, "Puerto Ricans and Education," *Journal of Teacher Education* 26 (Summer 1975): 128–30; and Carlos Munoz, Jr., *Youth, Identity, Power: The Chicano Movement* (New York: Verso, 1990).

26. Several scholars argue that the inclusion of native language instruction in the definition of bilingual education was influenced by bilingual programs in Dade County, Florida, which were founded to address the needs of the first wave of middle class Cuban immigrants. These immigrants saw themselves as temporary residents of the United States who would soon return to their country and therefore wanted to preserve their culture and language. The success of these programs gave encouragement

to the idea of bilingual education as a method of instruction for students from disadvantaged backgrounds. See U. Casanova, "Bilingual Education: Politics or Pedagogy," in O. Garcia ed., *Bilingual Education,* Vol 1. (Amsterdam: John Benjamins Publishing Company, 1991), 167–82; Kenji Hakuta, *Mirror of Language* (New York: Basic Books, 1986).

27. *Public Law 93–380,* Aug. 21, 1974, Sec. 702(a.)(5).

28. "Memorandum of Frank Carlucci, Under Secretary of Education, to the Assistant Secretary for Education, December 2, 1974," In *Bilingual Education: An Unmet Need— Report to the Congress by the Comptroller General of the United States* (Washington, D.C.: Comptroller General of the United States, May 1976), 56.

29. This argument was made by Wiese and García in 1998. See Ann-Marie Wiese and Eugene E. García, "The Bilingual Education Act: Language Minority Students and Equal Educational Opportunity," *Bilingual Research Journal* 22:1 (Winter 1998): 1–13.

30. *Public Law 95-561,* Nov. 1, 1978 Sec. 703 a4A & B.

31. For several examples of research studies documenting the primacy of learning English in bilingual education see Rolf Kjolseth, "Bilingual Education Programs in the United States: Assimilation or Pluralism?" in Bernard Spolsky, ed., *The Language Education of Minority Children* (Rowley, MA: Newbury House Publishers, Inc., 1972), 94–121; A. Bruce Gaarder, "The First Seventy-six Bilingual Education Projects," in James E. Alatis, ed., *Bilingualism and Language Contact* (Washington, D.C.: Georgetown University Press, 1970), 163–78; Jose Cardenas in Noel Epstein, *Language, Ethnicity and the Schools* (Washington, D.C.: Institute for Educational Leadership, 1977), 73.

32. The most important lawsuit was *Lau v. Nichols,* 414 U.S. 563. This landmark case laid the legal basis for bilingual education and is discussed in a variety of legal and nonlegal journals. See for instance, Christopher Reeber, "Linguistic Minorities and the Right to an Effective Education," *California Western International Law Journal* 3 (1972): 112–32; U.S. Civil Rights Commission, "The Constitutional Right to Non-English speaking Children to Equal Educational Opportunity," in *A Better Chance to Learn: Bilingual-Bicultural Education* (Washington, D.C.: GPO, 1975), 142–70; E. Grubb, "Breaking the Language Barrier: The Right to Bilingual Education," *Harvard Civil Rights-Civil Liberties Law Review,* 9 (1974): 52–94; W. Johnson, "The Constitutional Right of Bilingual Children to an Equal Educational Opportunity," *Southern California Law Review* 47:3 (May 1974): 943–97; and Joseph Montoya, "Bilingual-Bicultural

Education: Making Equal Educational Oportunity Available to National Origin Minority Children," *Georgetown University Law Journal* 61 (1973): 991–1007.

33. In 1974, Congress also passed the Equal Educational Opportunity Act, a piece of congressional legislation that, among other things, mandated local school districts to take affirmative steps to deal with the language needs of minority group children. This also served as another legal mandate. The section dealing with language was Title II of this act. See Equal Educational Opportunity Act of 1974, *Public Law 93–380*, sec. 204 f.

34. *Lau v. Nichols*, 414 U.S. 563, 94 S. Ct. 786 (1974).

35. J. Stanley Pottinger, *Memorandum of May 25, 1970 to School Districts with More than Five Percent National Origin-Minority Group Children* (Washington, D.C.: Department of Health, Education, and Welfare, Office for Civil Rights, 1970). For a history of the making of this memo see Martin H. Gerry, "Cultural Freedom in the Schools: The Right of Mexican-American Children to Succeed," in Alfredo Castaneda, et al., eds., *Mexican Americans and Educational Change* (New York: Arno Press, 1974), 226–55.

36. Pottinger, *Memorandum of May 25*.

37. Office for Civil Rights, *Task Force Findings Specifying Remedies Available for Eliminating Past Educational Practices Ruled Unlawful under Lau v. Nichols* (Washington, D.C.: Department of Health, Education, and Welfare, Office for Civil Rights, 1975). Quotations appear on pp. 6 and 7.

38. For information on the status of bilingual education legislation, implementation, and compliance with the *Lau* Remedies during the latter part of the 1970s and early 1980s see *Strengthening Bilingual Education: A Report from the Commissioner of Education to the Congress and the President* (Washington, D.C.: USOE, DHEW, June 1979) and *The Condition of Bilingual Education in the Nation, 1984: A Report from the Secretary of Education to the President and the Congress* (Washington, D.C.: USDOE, 1984).

39. See Susan Gilbert Schneider, *Revolution, Reaction or Reform: The 1974 Bilingual Education Act* (New York: L.A. Publishing Company, 1976).

40. The Voting Rights Act of 1975, *Public Law 94–73*, Aug 6, 1975, 89 Stat. 400.

41. I might note that the first state to enact a mandatory bilingual education act was Massachusetts. See M. Geffert et al., *The Current Status of U.S. Bilingual Education Legislation* (Arlington, VA: Center for Applied Linguistics, 1975).

42. *Development Associates, Inc., Final Report on a Study of State Programs in Bilingual Education* (Washington, D.C.: Office of Planning, Budget, and Evaluation, Office of Education, Department of Health, Education, and Welfare, 1977); and NACBE, "State Legislation on Bilingual Education," in *Fourth Annual Report* (Washington, D.C.: National Advisory Council on bilingual Education, 1979), 99–146. For an overview of these developments see Crawford, *Bilingual Education: History, Politics, Theory, and Practice* (Trenton, NJ: Crane Publishing Co., 1989), 33.

43. Crawford, *Bilingual Education,* 33.

44. Ariz Rev. Stat. Ann. Sec. 15–202, Supp. May 1969, quoted in Arnold Leibowitz, "English Literacy: Legal Sanction for Discrimination," *Notre Dame Lawyer* 45:7 (Fall 1969): 7–67. Quotation is from page 51.

45. See Crawford, *Bilingual Education,* 33.

46. For one example of how the advertising industry has been increasing its Spanish language ads during the 1980s see Jube Shiver, Jr., "Ad Industry Learns to Say It In Spanish," *Los Angeles Times,* 7 June 1987, Part IV, p. 1.

47. Gilbert Sanchez, "An Analysis of the Bilingual Education Act, 1967–1968," (Ph.D. diss., University of Massachusetts, 1973); Elliot Lewis Judd, "Factors Affecting the Passage of the Bilingual Education Act of 1967," (Ph.D. diss., New York University, 1977).

48. For an overview of their role, see Rodolfo Rodríguez, "Citizen Participation in ESEA Title VII Programs: An Inquiry into the Impact of a Federal Mandate," (pp. 260–280) and Norberto Cruz, Jr., "Roles, Functions and Compliance of Parent Advisory Councils Serving Spanish-English Bilingual Projects Funded Under ESEA Title VII," (pp. 281–294) in Raymond V. Padilla, ed., *Bilingual Education and Public Policy in the United States* (Ypsilanti, MI: Department of Foreign Languages and Bilingual Studies, Eastern Michigan University, 1979).

49. Sanchez, "An Analysis;" Elliot Lewis Judd, "Factors Affecting the Passage."

50. *Bilingual Education—An Unmet Need* (Washington, D.C.: GPO, 1976).

51. *Lau v. Nichols,* 414 U.S. 563. For overviews of these judicial developments see *Bilingual Education: Current Perspectives, Vol. 3–Law* (Arlington, VA: Center for Applied Linguistics, 1973); W. Foster, "Bilingual Education: An Educational and Legal Survey," *Journal of Law and Education* 5 (1976): 149–71; Peter D. Roos, "Bilingual Education: Hispanic Response to Unequal Education," *Law and Contemporary Problems* 42 (1978): 111–40; and Herbert Teitelbaum and Richard J. Hiller, "Bilingual Education: The Legal Mandate," *Harvard Educational Review* 47 (May 1977): 138–70.

52. Noel Epstein, *Language, Ethnicity and the Schools: Policy Alternatives for Bilingual-Bicultural Education* (Washington, D.C.: Institute for Educational Leadership, 1977), 1.

53. Epstein, *Language,* 27.

54. Epstein, *Language,* 19–20.

55. He critiqued three major arguments—that there is no federal legal requirement for bilingual education, that bilingual education is a Hispanic separatist movement, and that English language immersion is a desireable and innovative alternative to bilingual education—and over ten minor ones. See Jose A. Cardenas, "Response I," in Noel Epstein, *Language,* 76–84.

56. Jose A. Cardenas, "Response I," 84.

57. Jose A. Cardenas, "Response I," 84.

58. Malcolm N. Danoff, *Evaluation of the Impact of ESEA Title VII Spanish/English Bilingual Education Programs* (Palo Alto, CA: American Institutes for Research, 1978).

59. See, for instance, Cannon, "Bilingual Problems," 452–58; and G. R. Tucker and Alison D'Anglesan, "Some Thoughts Concerning Bilingual Education Programs," *Modern Language Journal* 55 (Dec 1971): 491–93.

60. General Accounting Office, *Summary Project of Type of Instruction Received by Students at 46 Schools Enrolled in 28 Bilingual Education Projects Reviewed by GAO* (Washington, D.C.: GPO, Feb 13, 1973).

61. U.S. Commission on Civil Rights, *The Excluded Student: Educational Practices Affecting Mexicans Americans in the Southwest. Report III: Mexican American Education Study* (Washington, D.C.: GPO, 1972).

62. Comptroller General "Factors Affecting Student Achievement," in *Bilingual Education—An Unmet Need,* (Washington, D.C.: GPO, 1976), 45–52.

63. Comptroller General "Factors," 45–52.

64. Cardenas, "Response I," 74. For other responses see Tracy C. Gray and M. Beatriz Arias, *Challenge to the AIR Report* (Arlington, VA: CAL, 1978); and Joan S. Bissell, *A Review of the Impact Study of ESEA Title VII Spanish/English Bilingual Education Programs* (Sacramento, CA: Office of the Auditor General, State Legislature, March 1979).

65. Robert A. Cervantes, *An Exemplary Consafic Chingatropic Assessment: The AIR Report* (Los Angeles: National Dissemination and Assessment Center, 1978).

CHAPTER 3

RETRENCHMENT AND REDEFINITION, 1980–1988

INTRODUCTION

During the 1980s, organized opposition to bilingual education policy grew significantly. Politicians, educators, scholars, and parent groups began to criticize bilingual education policies and programs at all levels of government and to call for their curtailment.

Several specific factors were responsible for the growth of this opposition. Among the specific factors were the changes in policy over time, the increased federal support of bilingual education methods, growing minority empowerment, and misunderstandings and ignorance of pedagogical methods concerning first and second language learning among language majority and minority students in the United States.

A variety of underlying factors also contributed to the emergence of organized opposition to bilingual education in this decade. One of these was the rise of conservatism in American life in general and the control by the Republican Party of the executive branch of the federal government in particular. In 1980, Ronald Reagan, a one-time film actor, former California governor, and staunch Republican, won by a landslide. Although he received 50.7% of the popular vote, he won 489 out of 538 electoral votes to become president of the United States. The election of Reagan to office initiated a significant shift in the federal government's support for bilingual education.[1] A primary objective of his administration was to limit the role of the federal government.[2] In keeping with this philosophy, Reagan and his allies halted the growth of bilingual education and significantly modified this policy and its implementation.

Other factors assisted opponents in reversing bilingual education advances, including the loss of nerve by liberal politicians to fight for their own ideals, the restlessness of the lay public over minority rights, domestic and international economic conditions, the rapid growth and changing nature of immigration, especially from non-European countries, the fragmentation of the left and progressive organizations, the growing presence and influence of non-English speaking groups on American culture, and the emergence of the U.S. English-only movement. This latter movement developed more stringent criticisms of the effectiveness of bilingual education, of the federal role, and of the need for native language instruction in bilingual programs. It also raised questions and concerns about the costs for establishing these programs, and about the number of children needing and being served by them.[3]

For the most part, those in opposition to this policy favored assimilation, English-only public policies, the limited participation of ethnic minorities in public policy, and compensatory school reforms, that is, reforms aimed specifically at targeted groups of individuals requiring special services. Many of them wanted to reverse the gains made by the supporters of bilingual education and halt the growth of bilingual education throughout the country. More specifically, they wanted to decrease or eliminate the use of non-English languages in public education and improve the academic achievement of low-income, limited-English-speaking children through the teaching of English only. Others wanted to eliminate the mandatory aspects of this policy and the federal preference for bilingual education or to promote Americanization instead of cultural pluralism in the schools.

Although contested, two major strategies were pursued by the opponents: an ideological one aimed at attacking the empirical basis of bilingual education and a political one of repealing or modifying federal bilingual education.

INCREASING ATTACKS AGAINST BILINGUAL EDUCATION

The first major strategy raised questions about the goals, effectiveness, and consequences of federal bilingual education. Its emphasis was on challenging the need for sustained native language instruction. The primary attack against bilingual education from the beginning was aimed at questioning its effectiveness. During the late 1970s, opponents began to argue that bilingual education was not effective in teaching limited-English-proficient (LEP) children English or in improving their academic achievement. Opponents also called for the enactment of a new policy that would consider alternatives to primary language instruction, especially English Immersion and English as a Second Language (ESL) approaches.[4] This emerging opposition was limited to a few individuals; it was not yet fully organized.

Serious opposition to bilingual education originated in 1981 with the appearance of several reports issued by the Office of Planning, Budget, and Evaluation (OPBE). This office, in response to a request by the Regulatory Analysis Review Group of the Council on Wage and Price Stability, prepared a series of studies in the latter part of this year that provided an "empirical" basis for challenging what two authors, Beatrice F. Birman and Alan L. Ginsburg, called "federal policy assumptions for language-minority children." According to them, federal policy was based on four basic assumptions that warranted reexamination:[5]

1. Approximately 3.6 million children needed bilingual education services.
2. If children from non-English-speaking backgrounds were not performing well in school, it was because of their dependence on the "home language."
3. Transitional bilingual education was the appropriate remedy for addressing the educational needs of language-minority children.
4. Federal policy could ignore local constraints such as the shortage of bilingual teachers, program costs, and the lack of language-proficiency tests.

The new studies prepared by the OPBE in October 1981 and published in book form two years later, challenged these assumptions. Each of them provided evidence questioning specific aspects of federal bilingual education policy.[6] Two of these studies, for instance, challenged assumption number one. One of them showed that the size of the language minority population eligible for federal services was smaller than had been estimated in prior years. More specifically, the author of this study, Robert E. Barnes, estimated that there were around 1 to 1.5 million, or only about one-third of the 3.6 million then used by the Department of Education.[7] Another study focused on the number of students being served by bilingual education programs. This study, conducted by Ann M. Milne and Jan M. Gombert, provided an analysis of OCR data and suggested that most of the children eligible for review under the Department's proposed rule of August 1980 were either already being served or in schools where their sparse population made language services difficult to provide.[8]

One particular study questioned the traditional linguistic explanation for low scholastic achievement among language minority groups. This study, done by Alvin S. Rosenthal, Ann M. Milne, Alan L. Ginsburg, and Keith A. Baker, argued that limited-English-speaking children did badly in school for a variety of reasons. Some of these, however, had little to do with their lack of English. According to Rosenthal, et al., some language minority students were already competent in English whereas others were limited in both languages, i.e., they were limited in their own native language as well as in English. Underachievement, they continued, also was due to factors other than language limitations, especially poverty.[9]

On the basis of these findings, Beatrice F. Birman and Alan L. Ginsburg, the two authors of an important policy study addressing the needs of language minority students, argued that if students were limited both in their native language and in English, the value of teaching them in two languages could be challenged. Likewise, if children's educational needs were based on factors other than language, bilingual programs could be only partial solutions. "From the perspective of the federal government," they concluded, "if students receive services that do not match their needs, federal funds are dissipated."[10]

Another study questioned the appropriateness of transitional bilingual education for addressing the educational needs of language minority children. This study became the most important one because of its influence in the debate over bilingual education. The authors of this report, Keith A. Baker and Adriana A. de Kanter, conducted a review of the literature on the effectiveness of bilingual education and found that bilingual education did not work as well as many believed it would.[11] They also argued that other approaches, especially immersion programs, were as effective as bilingual education. Birman and Ginsburg agreed with their findings and argued that "the case for the effectiveness of TBE (transitional bilingual education) is not overwhelming and should not warrant sole reliance on this approach to the exclusion of others."[12]

Finally, Birman and Ginsburg cited several studies that raised questions about the serious financial, personnel, and assessment constraints inhibiting the ability of local school districts to provide services. One of these constraints was cost. It was extremely costly, they noted, to establish bilingual education programs. This statement was based on a study done by Polly Carpenter-Huffman and Marta Samulon. These individuals argued that it took between $200 and $700 per child beyond existing costs to establish and maintain a bilingual education program. If 1.2 million children needed special language services the cost would be about $240 to $840 million to serve all the eligible children.[13] In an era of limited resources, Birman and Ginsburg noted, bilingual education became a luxury.

Schools also needed fully qualified staff but there was a lack of bilingual teachers. According to Elizabeth R. Reisner, the author of a study on the availability of bilingual education teachers, there was a 13,000 shortfall in the supply of trained personnel.[14] The lack of adequate tests to assess the children's own language proficiency likewise increased the possibility that the educational needs of language minority children could be misdiagnosed. This, in turn, could lead to the delivery of ineffective services.

Birman and Ginsburg noted that the OPBE studies did not dispute the need for "some sort of educational assistance" to meet the needs of language minority children. But they did argue that "in the process of justifying Federal support of bilingual education, too little attention has been paid to accurately identifying which children need services, which types of services would benefit them the most, and what constraints local school districts face in providing such services."[15]

In light of the new studies providing "systematic empirical evidence from a variety of data sources," Birman and Ginsburg argued that the continued federal support for bilingual education warranted reexamination. In their conclusion, they made the following policy recommendations: (1.) transitional bilingual education should not be the sole approach encouraged by federal policy, (2.) state and school districts should have greater discretion to decide which type of special program is most appropriate for their unique settings, (3.) the constraints facing states and districts in providing services to language minority children should not be ignored, and (4.) improved bilingual research and program evaluations should be conducted.[16]

The set of studies issued by the OPBE laid the basis for a comprehensive attack against bilingual education within the federal government. Soon, different federal agencies began to use these arguments to undermine the rationale for bilingual education and for federal support of this policy. The Office of the Inspector General (IG) initiated the attack against bilingual education in the 1980s. In 1982, the IG issued several reports critical of bilingual education in Texas. These reports, unlike most other IG audits, did not focus on issues of "waste, fraud, and abuse" but rather on more general issues of policy and program implementation. Seven school districts in Texas were chosen for program review. These audits found the following: the Title VII programs reviewed were ineffective (program evaluations showed that most did not meet the objectives stated in the application), the bilingual projects did not permanently improve the capacity of school districts (most money was spent on temporary teacher aides), an excessive number of non-LEP students participated in the programs (based on language dominance rather than proficiency measures), and the Texas Education Agency did not effectively coordinate local Title VII programs with other Federal and State programs serving LEP students.[17]

On the basis of these audits, the IG recommended that the seven Texas districts and the TEA refund $5,858,231 to the federal government. Such a refund was more than the seven districts and the TEA received in 1980–1981 ($3,690,140) and equaled forty-two percent of their cumulative grants under Title VII.[18]

Texas school officials contested the audit findings, challenged the validity of the "facts" cited in the audit reports, and charged that the Inspector General had utilized erroneous statutory and programmatic standards in preparing the reports. Congressional members also conducted an oversight hearing on these reports and threatened to pass legislation aimed at curtailing the power of the IG unless the Education Department dropped the disputed Texas audit recommendations.[19]

In 1985, the new secretary of education, William Bennett, joined the federal opponents in attacking and opposing bilingual education policy. In a major speech to the nation, he argued that bilingual education had gone astray and was not reaching its goal of teaching LEP children English.[20] Soon journalists, scholars, special interest groups, community organizations, and educators were attacking bilingual education and echoing the federal government's findings that it was not an effective means for teaching English to LEP children. They also clamored for changes in this policy.

The proponents of bilingual education responded to the attacks on their program during the 1980s. Most of them concentrated on the issue of effectiveness in general or on challenging the findings of the Baker/de Kanter report in particular.

There were at least three different types of responses to this report. First, researchers and proponents of bilingual education criticized the report's methodological flaws and its conclusions.[21] Second, educators began exploring, in more systematic fashion, the structured immersion method and ESL methods and their applicability to the education of LEP children in the United States.[22] A few scholars such as Eduardo

Hernandez-Chavez, however, presented compelling reasons for rejecting English-only methods as possible alternatives to bilingual education for LEP children.[23] The third response was to challenge the Baker/de Kanter study by reanalyzing the data that they had used. In the fall of 1985 Ann Willig conducted such a review of select studies on bilingual education. Unlike Baker/de Kanter's, her review indicated that bilingual education programs had greater impact on language and knowledge acquisition for LEP children than those failing to utilize the native language.[24]

The scholarly community also responded. In 1985, for instance, it issued two reports critical of the federal government's attack on bilingual education. One of these blamed the lack of bilingual services for poor achievement test scores in reading. The authors of the report, especially the principal author Joan Baratz, showed that language minority children, especially Hispanics, scored poorly in the National Assessment of Educational Progress' (NAEP) 1983–1984 reading assessment of fourth, eighth, and eleventh graders. She argued that one of the reasons for this low score was the lack of participation by language minority students in bilingual and ESL programs.[25] Although pressured to repudiate or at least modify some of the conclusions, Baratz' report undercut the high profile "initiative" by Secretary of Education Bennett to promote alternatives to bilingual instruction.

The second and probably most important document issued in 1985 was a formal evaluation study of bilingual education sponsored by the Department of Education. Known as *The Longitudinal Study of Immersion and Dual Language Instruction Programs for Language Minority Children,* this study's principal objectives were to provide a description of the structured immersion approach in the United States and to obtain information that would permit a comparison of the immersion and transitional bilingual education programs for helping LEP children to perform in English-only classrooms. This four-year longitudinal study by S.R.A. Technologies, Inc., was to be completed in September of 1988. Although this study had not been completed, first-year results were issued in December 1985. This study compared about 4,000 LEP kindergartners, first graders, and third graders enrolled in immersion classes, "early-exit"

or transitional bilingual education and "late-exit" or bilingual maintenance programs. It found that LEP students in bilingual programs consistently outperformed "immersion strategy" students in reading, language
arts, and mathematics tests conducted in both English and Spanish. English immersion, the instructional alternative that was popular among
critics of bilingual education, in other words, fared poorly in the Department of Education's first large-scale evaluation of the method.[26]

Congressional and government supporters of bilingual education
likewise issued their own reports in opposition to the critics. In the summer of 1986, Congressman Augustus F. Hawkins issued a report critical
of the series of studies published by the OPBE aimed at undermining
bilingual education research. Hawkins' report provided "empirical" evidence on the size of the LEP population and the effectiveness of bilingual
education, quantified the need for bilingual teachers, and provided data
on the academic achievement of these children and their need for more
rather than less native language instruction.[27]

The following year, another federal agency—the General Accounting
Office (GAO)—responded to Bennett's and Baker/de Kanter's charges of
bilingual education's ineffectiveness. This report provided an informal
evaluation of the federal government's statements about research. It
found that the Education Department's primary conclusion about bilingual education—that native language instruction had been proven no
more effective than "English-only" approaches—was unsupported by the
research evidence cited by the department. The GAO report, according
to Mr. Hawkins' aide, showed that "the Administration's position is ideological, rather than based on factual evidence."[28]

While the majority of the opponents argued that bilingual education
was not teaching English, others maintained that it was teaching other
things besides the national language. More specifically, they argued that
bilingual education was not assimilating immigrant children as fast as
it could. Instead of teaching American culture, bilingual education was
teaching immigrant and ethnic cultures or multiculturalism. In doing
so, it was promoting Hispanic separatism, cultural apartheid, linguistic segregation, and divisions based on language and culture. Bilingual

education, in other words, was creating a "Balkanized" society that could only lead to social fragmentation and ethnic conflict.[29]

A few critics argued that bilingual education was not an educational program but an affirmative action program for Latinos. "The bilingual education program is more or less the Hispanic equivalent of affirmative action, creating jobs for thousands of Spanish teachers; by which I mean teachers who speak Spanish, although not necessarily English, it has turned out," noted Tom Bethel, a conservative newspaper columnist. This jobs program, according to him, not only appealed to teachers of Spanish and other languages, but also "to those who never did think that another idea, the United States of America, was a particularly good one to begin with, and that the sooner it is restored to its component 'ethnic' parts, the better off we shall all be."[30]

Opponents also questioned the federal role in bilingual education. However, unlike during the 1970s when those opposed to bilingual education faulted the federal government for promoting private over public goals, in the 1980s they criticized it for being dictatorial, heavy-handed, or intrusive.[31] Regardless of the extent of involvement, critics of bilingual education argued that the federal government was now "dictating" the curriculum at the local level by mandating one single approach to educating LEP children.[32] The proper role of the federal government, noted an editorial in the *Washington Post* in 1980, was to see that the goal of providing equal opportunity was reached, not to prescribe the route that had to be taken.[33]

The remedy for these new ills, many opponents argued, was to curtail the federal role in bilingual education and to limit the amount of primary language instruction and information on minority cultures. Teaching English and Americanism, not bilingualism or multiculturalism, became the key ideals of the critics of bilingual education.

Those involved in the English-only movement also voiced their criticism and opposition to bilingual education. This movement originated in the early 1980s when former Senator S. I. Hayakawa of California teamed up with Dr. John Tanton, a Michigan ophthalmologist, environmentalist, and population control activist to establish the organization they called U.S. English. Soon other English-only organizations were founded.

The English-only movement argued that the English language was being threatened in the U.S. by immigrants who refused to learn it and by bilingual education. More specifically, those involved in this movement made several arguments:

1. English has been the country's "social glue," its most important "common bond," which has allowed Americans of diverse backgrounds to understand each other and overcome differences.
2. Today's immigrants refuse to learn English, unlike the immigrants of the past, or they are discouraged from doing so by government-sponsored bilingual programs.
3. Languages are best learned in a situation where one is forced to do so, where there is no escape from brutal necessity, unlike the situation in a bilingual classroom.
4. Ethnic leaders are promoting bilingualism for selfish ends: to provide jobs for their constituents and keep them dependent by discouraging them from learning English.
5. Language diversity inevitably leads to language conflict, ethnic hostility, and political separatism as in Quebec.[34]

These arguments, noted James Crawford, a critic of the English-only movement, were all "demonstrably false." "Virtually no evidence has been produced on behalf of any of these propositions," he further noted.[35] English-only proponents, however, did not need facts to advance their cause. Emotionalism, crass opportunism, and ethnocentrism sustained them over time.[36]

This movement, while publicly in support of English, had a covert agenda. It was against the growing cultural and racial diversity of American society and tried to limit its growth. Its campaign, in other words, was not simply aimed at promoting English but at limiting linguistic and cultural pluralism.[37] During the 1980s, the English-only movement spearheaded the campaign for official-English and anti-bilingual legislation in

Congress and in state legislatures and ballot initiatives throughout the country. Because of its national membership, it played an influential role in developing arguments against federal bilingual education and in helping to repeal or modify this policy.

UNDERMINING POLICY AND PRACTICE

The diverse opposition not only questioned various aspects of federal bilingual education, it sought legislative and administrative changes in this policy, in its funding, and in the federal government's role. The supporters of bilingual education also contested these actions.

Opposition within the federal government came primarily from elected officials in the executive and legislative branch of government. The former I refer to as executive opponents, the latter as congressional opponents.

Executive opponents, led by two Republican presidents, guided the efforts to weaken federal support for bilingual education. Ronald Reagan initiated the campaign against bilingual education in 1980.[38] A primary objective of his administration was to limit the role of the federal government.[39] In keeping with this philosophy, Reagan and his congressional allies mounted an attack against bilingual education.[40]

Reagan initially tried to halt the growth of bilingual education by seeking rescissions and decreased funding. Between 1978 and 1984, funding for bilingual education decreased from a high of $158 million in 1979 to less than $133 million in 1986.[41] The number of basic programs increased from 565 to 589 but there was a decrease in the number of individuals being served. In 1978, before Reagan assumed power, slightly over 300,000 LEP students were being served. By the end of Reagan's first term in 1984, the number participating in bilingual education programs had decreased to 182,000.[42]

Funding during the years from 1984 to 1986 remained fairly constant at $132 million. In the 1986–1987 fiscal year, however, the funding level for the bilingual education act increased to $143 million. The need for Latino votes in the presidential elections and the wooing of Latino voters by the Republican Party led to this increase.[43]

Reagan also eliminated the mandatory provisions of bilingual education by dismantling the civil rights component of this federal program. Several months after his inauguration he urged the Department of Education to withdraw the proposed federal guidelines for ensuring compliance with non-discrimination policies. The proposed guidelines had been issued in early 1980 by President Jimmy Carter, a Democrat, in anticipation of gaining Hispanic votes in the upcoming presidential elections and in response to a federal court decision. They provided guidance to local school districts on their responsibilities towards language minority children.[44] Those opposed to bilingual education, however, perceived the proposed remedies as extremely intrusive and as unworkable. The publication of these guidelines only served to inflame their passions and contributed to the defeat of the Democrats in the 1980 elections and the election of Reagan to the presidency and of Republicans to Congress.[45]

In order to make a point about the government's new direction and in keeping with his conservative philosophy, President Reagan, as noted above, withdrew the proposed *Lau* Remedies in February 1981.[46] Fourteen months later, in April 1982 the secretary of education withdrew the existing *Lau* Remedies. According to David G. Savage, a *Los Angeles Times* journalist, conservatives quietly applauded while advocates only provided muted protests to this policy shift.[47]

At the beginning of his second term, President Reagan developed a new initiative to undermine bilingual education policy. He appointed William J. Bennett, an avid opponent of bilingual education, to head the Department of Education in 1985 and to lead this initiative against native language instruction in public education. Once in office, Bennett developed a coherent plan to redirect the program towards more English instruction.[48]

First, the Department of Education under Bennett developed new regulations aimed at promoting local flexibility in bilingual program design and at eliminating the use of non-English language instruction in these programs. The new regulations, formulated in 1985, reflected the conservative ideology of the Reagan administration. They provided specific guidelines for implementing the provisions of the 1984 bilingual education bill. According to these regulations, school districts could, among other actions, decrease the amount of native language instruction provided in their federally funded programs.[49]

Latino groups assailed these bilingual education regulations and argued that they would negatively impact the schooling of language minority children.[50] Their opposition had no significant impact on the regulations.

Several months after their development, James Crawford reported that a review of the comments and letters to the proposed regulations indicated that most of those expressing support for the department's policy opposed bilingual education in any form. Many also expressed ethnic animosities towards language minorities, especially Hispanics.[51] In April 1986, the federal government issued a final set of regulations. No major changes had been made.[52]

Second, Bennett downgraded the primary instrument for enforcing the *Lau* decision—the Office for Civil Rights—by drastically reducing its budget and staff.[53] More specifically, he reduced the funding for enforcement compliance, decreased the number of investigations of school districts with inadequate bilingual programs, and failed to investigate complaints of discrimination.

Finally, he sought to undo existing *Lau* agreements. In November 1985, Bennett invited more than 400 school districts to renegotiate long-standing agreements governing their curricula for LEP students.[54] Critics of Bennett's initiative argued that few districts would take up the government's offer because "it would be a tremendous administrative burden to re-tool entire programs."[55] These critics were correct. Within the next three years, only fourteen, or three percent, of the nation's 498 districts agreed to modify their *Lau* plans and most of these involved minor, technical modifications.[56]

These actions served to effectively dismantle the civil rights component of this program and to weaken the mandatory provisions of federal bilingual education. By June 1986, James Crawford, a proponent of bilingual education and a reporter for *Education Week*, noted that due to Reagan's actions, the federal efforts to ensure equal access to the curriculum by language minority children had declined steadily over the past five years. This finding, coupled with Bennett's invitation to renegotiate the *Lau* plans, only added to the public perception that few efforts were being made to enforce civil rights provisions.[57]

Bennett likewise took a variety of administrative actions aimed at weakening the administration of bilingual education. For instance, he sought to dismantle the National Clearinghouse on Bilingual Education by defunding it and by awarding the contract to another group less supportive of bilingual education. Additionally, he modified criteria in order to award funds to those utilizing English-only approaches and limited funding to Title VII training institutes only.[58] Finally, he appointed several individuals opposed to bilingual education to the newly structured National Advisory and Coordinating Council on Bilingual Education (NACCBE).[59]

The response by the supporters of bilingual education to Bennett's initiative was rapid and critical. Many of these individuals criticized him for his shortsightedness and the negative implications his strategy could have on language minority children.[60] Bennett's ideas on bilingual education, however, were soon incorporated into and reflected in his proposed regulations, legislative proposals, and administrative actions.

Congressional opponents also took a variety of actions against bilingual education. Between 1980 and 1988 some of them tried to repeal bilingual education through various means. A few congresspersons introduced bills aimed at eliminating the Bilingual Education Act whereas others introduced English-only legislation in the hopes that it would outlaw the use of non-English languages in public policy. For example, in addition to various statutes and resolutions pertaining to the English language, sixteen amendments were introduced in the U.S. Congress between 1981 and 1990. Some of these amendments were simply one-liners establishing English as the nation's official language. Others were English-only mandates outlawing the uses of other languages by federal, state, and local governments. None of them became law.[61]

Unable to repeal bilingual education, congressional opponents reverted to the strategy of modifying it. As early as 1978, congressional opponents fought for several important changes to bilingual education policy, many of which were counteracted by supporters of this program. In this year, the latter managed to expand the scope and funding of bilingual education. Congressional supporters broadened the definition of the children eligible for participation in the program from "limited English speaking" to "limited English proficient." This provision expanded the number of individuals from those who had difficulty in speaking and understanding English to include those who also had difficulty in reading and writing the same language. The amendments to the bilingual education act also committed substantial funds for research, teacher preparation, and graduate fellowships and allowed English speakers to participate in this program.[62]

Although unable to halt the expansion of bilingual education, the opponents, largely led by Republican legislators, won several significant concessions in this reauthorization effort. They got Congress to underscore the importance of becoming proficient in English and to deemphasize the use of the primary language or of the culture in the instructional program. Funding was also largely limited to accomplishing this goal.[63]

In addition to this emphasis on achieving competency in the English language, a new provision was added stipulating that the commissioner could issue an order to terminate federal funding of bilingual programs for those local school districts not having long-term needs for continued assistance under the amended act. Another provision was also added which required that applicants demonstrate that federal grants would gradually be replaced by local or state funds to help achieve a regularly funded program. Finally, congressional opponents added a ceiling of forty percent to the percentage of English speakers who could participate in bilingual education programs.[64]

During the next decade, the opponents of bilingual education fought for and successfully made further changes to this policy. They placed limits on the number of years LEP children could participate in bilingual programs (two to three years), on the number of English-speaking children eligible to participate (from forty percent of the total to none), and on the amount of non-English languages one could use in bilingual education (less than half a day; less than one hour per day). Ironically, while they limited the types of students who could enroll in bilingual education programs, opponents expanded the coverage to include the diverse groups of immigrants coming to this country, especially those from Latin America, the Caribbean, and Asia.[65]

Although all of these changes impacted the character of bilingual education, none was more significant than the redefinition of this policy allowing the funding of English-only alternatives to native language instruction. In 1978 only bilingual education programs were fundable.[66] In 1984, federal policy allowed an English-only alternative to native language instruction.[67] Officially, five programs were fundable. Three of these were instructional programs for LEP children: Transitional Bilingual Education (TBE), Developmental Bilingual Education (DBE), and Special Alternative Instructional Programs (SAIP). The first two allowed for native language instruction; the latter did not. In defense of the program, supporters of bilingual education managed to insert a provision stipulating that only ten percent of total funds for this policy could be used for this English-only method.[68] In 1988 this policy was amended to allow up to twenty-five percent of total bilingual education funds for establishing English-only instructional programs. The amended bill also stipulated that one hundred percent of any new funds above $130 million had to be devoted to English-only methods.[69]

Although the funding for English language programs was increased to twenty-five percent of total funds for bilingual education in 1988, during the next dozen years, congressional opponents sought to increase the percentage of funding that went to English-only approaches.

CONCLUSION

Although present for many years, opposition to bilingual education did not emerge until the late 1970s. At first, it was highly unorganized and limited primarily to journalists and researchers. In the 1980s, the president of the United States, a few specific federal agencies, Republican officeholders, and special interest groups, especially English-only organizations joined the battle against bilingual education in particular and against the increased federal role in education in general. Although contested, this opposition developed a comprehensive rationale against the use of native language instruction, halted the growth of bilingual education and began to gradually modify this policy and the federal government's preference for it. Additional changes would be made to bilingual education in the following decade as conservative forces strengthened their hold on American life in general and on the federal government in particular.

NOTES

1. Ornstein argues, for instance, that there were three basic trends in federal education policy during the Reagan administration's first term: a shift in priorities from social to military and business concerns, reduction in federal funds for education, and a growing demise of the goal of egalitarianism as a national policy. See Allan C. Ornstein, "The Changing Federal Role in Education," *American Education* 20 (December 1984): 4–7. See also Jack H. Shuster, "Out of the Frying Pan: The Politics of Education in a New Era," *Phi Delta Kappan* (May 1982): 583–91.

2. Ira Shor, *Culture Wars: School and Society in the Conservative Restoration, 1969–1984* (NY: Routledge and Kegan Paul, 1986).

3. For a history of English-only movements in the U.S. see James Crawford, *Hold Your Tongue: Bilingualism and the Politics of "English Only"* (New York: Addison-Wesley Publishing Company, 1992). See also James Crawford, ed., *Language Loyalties: A Source Book on the Official English Controversy* (Chicago: University of Chicago Press, 1992).

4. See, for instance, Malcolm N. Danoff, *Evaluation of the Impact of ESEA Title VII Spanish/English Bilingual Education Programs* (Palo Alto, CA: AIR, 1978). For a critique of the AIR reports see Jose Cardenas, "Response I," in Noel E. Epstein, *Language, Ethnicity and the Schools* (Washington, D.C.: Institute for Educational Leadership, 1977), 71–84; Tracy C. Gray and M. Beatriz Arias, *Challenge to the AIR Report* (Arlington, VA: Center for Applied Linguistics, 1978); Joan S. Bissell, *A Review of the Impact Study of ESEA Title VII Spanish/English Bilingual Education Programs* (Sacramento, CA: Office of the Auditor General, State Legislature, 1979); and Robert A. Cervantes, *An Exemplary Consafic Chingatropic Assessment: The AIR Report* (Los Angeles: National Dissemination and Assessment Center, 1978).

5. Beatrice F. Birman and Alan L. Ginsburg, "Introduction: Addressing the Needs of Language-Minority Children," in Keith A. Baker and Adriana A. de Kanter, eds., *Bilingual Education: A Reappraisal of Federal Policy* (Lexington, MA: D.C. Heath and Company, 1983), xv.

6. Birman and Ginsburg, "Introduction," xv.

7. Robert E. Barnes, *Size of the Eligible Language Minority Population* (Washington, D.C.: OPBE, 1981).

8. Ann M. Milne and Jan M. Gombert, *Students with Primary Language Other Than English: Distribution and Service Rates* (Washington, D.C.: OPBE, 1981).

9. See Alvin S. Rosenthal, Ann M. Milne, Alan L. Ginsburg, Keith A. Baker, *A Comparison of the Effects of Language Background and Socio-Economic Status on Achievement Among Elementary School Students* (Washington, D.C.: OPBE, 1981).

10. Birman and Ginsburg, "Introduction," xvi.

11. Baker and de Kanter, *Effectiveness.*

12. Beatrice F. Birman and Alan L. Ginsburg, *Addressing the Needs of Language Minority Children: Issues for Federal Policy* (Washington, D.C.: OPBE, 1981), xvi.

13. Polly Carpenter-Huffman and Marta Samulon, *Case Studies of Delivery and Cost of Bilingual Education* (Washington, D.C.: OPBE, 1981).

14. See Elizabeth R. Reisner, *The Availability of Bilingual Education Teachers: Implications for Title VI Enforcement and Good Educational Practice* (Washington, D. C.: OPBE, 1981).

15. Birman and Ginsburg, *Addressing the Needs,* xiv. See also Keith A. Baker and Adriana A. de Kanter, eds., *Bilingual Education: A Reappraisal of Federal Policy* (Lexington, MA: Lexington Books, 1983).

16. These policy recommendations were slightly modified in the 1983 book. See Birman and Ginsburg, "Introduction," xix.

17. Inspector General, *Review of Federal Bilingual Education Programs in Texas* (Washington, D.C.: GPO, 1982).

18. Ibid.

19. See U.S. Congress, House, Education and Labor, *Committee on Oversight on Texas Bilingual Education Audits* (Washington, D.C.: GPO, July 29, 1982).

20. *Address by William J. Bennett, U.S. Secretary of Education to the Association for a Better New York,* New York, New York, September 26, 1985. In author's possession.

21. Eduardo Hernandez-Chavez, Jose Llanes, Roberto Alvarez, and Steve Arvizu, *The Federal Policy Toward Language and Education: Pendulum or Progress?* Monograph

No. 12 (Sacramento, CA: Cross Cultural Resource Center, California State University, 1981); Stanley S. Seidner, *Political Expediency or Educational Research: An Analysis of Baker and de Kanter's Review of the Literature of Bilingual Education* (Rosslyn, VA: National Clearinghouse for Bilingual Education, 1981).

22. *Studies in Immersion* (Sacramento, CA: California State Department of Education, l984). See also Fred Genovese, "The Suitability of Immersion Programs for All Children," *Canadian Modern Language Review* 32 (1976): 494–515.

23. Eduardo Hernandez-Chavez, "The Inadequacy of English Immersion Education as an Educational Approach for Language Minority Students in the United States," *Studies in Immersion* (Sacramento, CA: California State Department of Education, 1984), 144–83. For a more balanced view on English methods, especially ESL, see Anna Uhl Chamot, *The English as a Second Language Literature* (ESLIT) Study (Arlington, VA: InterAmerica Research Associates, Inc., 1985).

24. Ann Willig, "A Meta-Analysis of Selected Studies on the Effectiveness of Bilingual Education," *Review of Educational Research* 55:3 (Fall 1985): 269–317.

25. *The Educational Progress of Language Minority Students: Findings from the 1983–1984 NAEP Reading Study* (Washington, D.C.: National Assessment of Educational Progress, December l985), summarized in James Crawford, "Finn Blasts NAEP's 'Misleading' Report on Bilingual Services," *Education Week,* 2 April 1986, p. 1, 14.

26. David Ramirez, *The Longitudinal Study of Immersion and Dual Language Instruction Programs for Language Minority Children* (Washington, D.C.: S.R.A. Technologies, Inc., December 1985).

27. Augustus F. Hawkins, Chair, Committee on Education and Labor in the House of Representatives. U.S., Congress, House, *A Report of the Compendium of Papers on the Topic of Bilingual Education of the Committee on Education and Labor,* 99th Congress, 2d Sess. (Washington, D.C.: GPO, June 1986).

28. "GAO Report Fires Latest Salvo in Capitol War over Bilingual Education," *Houston Chronicle,* 9 Nov. 1986, 32A. See also U.S. General Accounting Office, *Bilingual Education: A New Look at the Research Evidence* (Washington, D.C.: GPO, March 1987).

29. Noel Epstein, *Language, Ethnicity and the Schools: Policy Alternatives for Bilingual-Bicultural Education* (Washington, D.C.: Institute for Educational Leadership, 1977). For an elaboration of these arguments see Rosalie Pedalino Porter, *Forked Tongue: The Politics of Bilingual Education* (New York: Basic Books, 1990).

30. Tom Bethel, "Why Johnny Can't Speak English," *Harper's,* February 1979, 28.

31. See, for instance, Epstein, *Language.*

32. See Max Rafferty, "Bilingual Education: Hoax of the 1980s," *The American Legion,* March 1981, 4, 15–16, 39–40; and William Raspberry, "No Sense—In Any Language," *Washington Post,* 22 October 1980, A23.

33. Editorial, "Drop the Bilingual Rules," *Washington Post,* 28 October 1980, A16.

34. James Crawford, "Anatomy of the English-Only Movement: Social and Ideological Sources of Language Restrictionism in the United States," in Douglas A. Kibbee, ed., *Language Legislation and Linguistic Rights* (Philadelphia: John Benjamins Publishing Company, 1998), 96–126.

35. James Crawford, "Anatomy," 98.

36. James Crawford, "Anatomy," 96–126. See also James Crawford, *At War With Diversity* (Buffalo, NY: Multilingual Matters, 2000).

37. James Crawford, "Anatomy," 114.

38. Ornstein, "Changing Federal Role," 4–7. See also Shuster, "Out of the Frying Pan," 583–91.

39. Shor, *Culture Wars.*

40. See Ornstein, "Changing Federal Role," 4–7; and Shuster, "Out of the Frying Pan," 583–91.

41. Bethel, "Why Johnny Can't," 28.

42. This data can be gleaned from the following reports: *Strengthening Bilingual Education: A Report from the Commissioner of Education to the Congress and the President* (Washington, D.C.: USOE, DHEW, June 1979) and *The Condition of Bilingual Education in the Nation, 1984: A Report from the Secretary of Education to the President and the Congress* (Washington, D.C.: USDOE, 1984).

43. National Advisory and Coordinating Council on Bilingual Education, *Tenth Annual Report* (Washington, D.C.: US Dept of Education, March 1986); James L. Lyons, "The View from Washington," *NABE News,* X(Fall 1986): 11, 15.

44. *Federal Register* 45, no. 152 (Tuesday, 5 August 1980): 52052–52076.

45. For opposition to the proposed *Lau* Remedies see Rafferty, "Bilingual Education;" Raspberry, "No Sense;" and Editorial, "Drop the Bilingual Rules."

46. For a sampling of the reasons for their withdrawal and the controversy this caused see "U.S. to Withdraw Bilingual Rules," *Corpus Christi Times,* 2 February 1981, 15; "Bell Acts to Withdraw Proposed Bilingual Education Guidelines," *Houston Chronicle,* 3

February 1981, 16B; and "Local Hispanics Rap Reagan's Bilingual Stand," *Corpus Christi Caller,* 3 March 1981, 38.

47. David G. Savage, "Bilingual Education Rules Lifted," *Los Angeles Times,* 25 April 1982, 1, 16–17.

48. *Address by William J. Bennett.*

49. "Notice of Proposed Rulemaking," *Federal Register,* 50, no. 226 (22 Nov. 1985): 48352–48370.

50. James Crawford, "Bennett's Plan for Bilingual Overhaul Heats Up Debate," *Education Week,* 12 February 1986, 1, 22; Lee May, "Latinos Assail Bilingual Education Plans," *Los Angeles Times,* 25 January 1986, part I, p. 3.

51. James Crawford, "Supporting Comments Reveal Animosity Toward Ethnic Groups," *Education Week,* 12 February 1986, 23.

52. These regulations can be found in "Bilingual Education Regulations," *Federal Register* 51, no. 118 (19 June 1986): 22422–22447. See also "Bilingual Education Regulations," *Federal Register* 51, no.180 (17 September 1986): 33000–33002.

53. For a detailed view of these and other actions illustrating "a declining federal leadership in promoting equal educational opportunity" between 1980 and 1982 see "U.S. Commission on Civil Rights Addresses Educational Inequities," *IDRA Newsletter* (April 1982): 1–8. A general interpretation of the changing nature of the federal role in education under the Reagan Administration is provided by Shuster, "Out of the Frying Pan," 583–91; and Ornstein, "Changing Federal Role," 4–7.

54. A copy of this action is found in "Text of Civil Rights Office Letters to Regional Heads, School Districts," *Education Week,* 27 Nov. 1985, 16. See also James Hertling, "Flexibility Stressed in New Rules for Bilingual Classes," *Education Week,* 27 Nov. 1985, 1, 16.

55. Hertling, "Flexibility," 16.

56. "Few Ask to Change 'Lau Plans,'" *Education Week,* 4 June 1988, p. 15.

57. Alan Brinkley, Richard N. Current, Frank Freidel, and T. Harry Williams, eds., *American History: A Survey, Volume II: Since 1865,* 8th ed., (New York: McGraw-Hill, Inc.), 962.

58. James Crawford, "Bilingual Program Grantees Told to Cut Travel, Salary Expenses," *Education Week,* 11 June 1986, 10; and "'Mainstreaming' Is Factor in Bilingual Grant Awards, Official Says," *Education Week,* 22 October 1986, 6.

59. The changes in membership, mandated by the 1984 bill, and the new directions in bilingual policy they sought to implement can be found in *Ninth Annual Report, 1984–1985* (Washington, D.C.: US Dept of Education, 1985) and in *Tenth Annual Report, 1985–1986* (Washington, D.C.: US Dept of Education, 1986).

60. See, for instance, Office of Research Advocacy and Legislation, *Secretary Bennett's Bilingual Education Initiative: Historical Perspectives and Implications* (Washington, D.C.: National Council of La Raza, Oct 31, 1985) and James L. Lyons, "Education Secretary Bennett on Bilingual Education: Mixed Up or Malicious?" *CABE Newsletter* 8:2 (October/November 1985): 1, 15.

61. For copies of four different official-English amendments to the U.S. Constitution introduced between 1981 and 1989, see James Crawford, ed., *Language Loyalties: A Source Book on the Official English Controversy* (Chicago: The University of Chicago Press, 1992), 112–13.

62. *Bilingual Education Act,* Public Law 95–561, 92 Stat.2268 (1978), Sec. 703.

63. *Bilingual Education Act,* Public Law 95–561, 92 Stat.2268 (1978) Sec. 703.

64. *Bilingual Education Act,* Public Law 95–561, 92 Stat.2268 (1978), Sec. 702; Sec 721.

65. *Bilingual Education Act,* Public Law 100–297, 102 Stat. 279 (1988), Part A.

66. *Bilingual Education Act,* Public Law 95–561, 92 Stat. 2268 (1978).

67. *Bilingual Education Act,* Public Law 98–511, 98 Stat. 2370 (1984).

68. Ibid.

69. *Bilingual Education Act,* Public Law 100–297, 102 Stat. 279 (1988).

CHAPTER 4

THE FINAL PUSH, 1990s

INTRODUCTION

Opposition to bilingual education decreased in the early 1990s, at least within the executive and legislative branch of the federal government. The constant need for Latino votes by the Republican Party as well as the election of a Democratic president blunted attacks against this policy in the first half of the 1990s. By mid-decade, however, organized opposition to bilingual education significantly increased throughout the country. The resurgence in opposition was due to several factors, including the reauthorization of the Bilingual Education Act of 1994, the Republican control of both houses of Congress during the 1994 elections, the state initiatives against bilingual education in California and Arizona, and public opinion polls indicating that most Americans, including apparently Latinos, opposed bilingual education.

Opponents became more diverse in this decade. In addition to conservative special interest groups such as the Republican Party, Anglo parent groups, administrators, assimilationists and U.S. English groups, they also included the following groups:

1. educational traditionalists: those who favored improved standards, rigorous accountability measures, and high stakes testing.
2. political opportunists: politicians, especially members of the Democratic Party, who changed their positions on important issues such as bilingual education in order to gain political favor with the dominant ruling groups and

3. los ignorantes (the ignorant ones): individuals who did not under-
    stand or who refused to understand that one of the primary
    purposes of bilingual education was to teach English as quickly
    as instructionally possible.

DECLINE AND RESURGENCE OF ATTACKS AGAINST BILINGUAL EDUCATION

Several important political reasons accounted for the decrease in opposition to bilingual education in the early 1990s. First, the George Bush
administration and the Republican Party needed to attract Latino voters
during the 1992 presidential election. One of the ways Republicans sought
to accomplish this was by taking a stand in support of bilingual education, an issue dear to many Latinos. In early 1991, President Bush took
such a stand when he issued the final results of a Department of Education study favoring bilingual education. This praise for bilingual education, noted one journalist, "was a marked shift from the stand of the
Reagan administration, which diverted funding from bilingual programs
at the urging of conservatives opposed to extensive native-language
instruction."[1]

The Department of Education in February 1991 released the findings of this research project, originally known as the Ramirez Report
(named after its principal investigator, J. David Ramirez). This comprehensive study compared the three most common methods of teaching
English Language Learners (ELLs): late-exit bilingual education, early-
exit bilingual education, and English immersion. In English immersion,
all instruction was conducted in English. Students in early-exit bilingual
education programs were taught in their native language for the first
three years of elementary schooling and then placed in regular English
language classrooms. Those in late-exit bilingual education programs
were taught in their native languages at least forty percent of the time
and stayed in the program through the sixth grade.

This study, begun during the Reagan administration in 1983, initially showed the relative success of late-exit bilingual education over

English-only methods. But the final results actually showed that all three methods worked. "Based on this study, we can conclude that bilingual education benefits students and school administrators can choose the method best suited to their students," said Ted Sanders, acting education secretary.[2]

Educators such as Rita Esquivel, the Department of Education's bilingual education director, said they hoped that the study would lay to rest the political storm over the use of native language instruction versus immersion programs in which only English was used. This study did no such thing. Bilingual advocates continued to believe that ELLs needed native language instruction to keep pace academically while learning English whereas opponents continued to believe that students should learn English as quickly as possible, without the use of their native language. Analysis of this report, in fact, showed that while all three methods were successful in teaching ELLs, the most effective of these methods was the late-exit model or the model utilizing the greatest amount of native language instruction.[3]

Opposition to bilingual education also decreased during the early 1990s as a result of the election of William Jefferson Clinton, a Democrat, to the presidency. President Clinton had campaigned in support of bilingual education and promised to strengthen it in a year in which Congress was expected to consider reauthorization of all elementary and secondary education programs, including the Bilingual Education Act. Bilingual educators, especially the members of the National Association of Bilingual Education (NABE), also felt that the public generally was more receptive toward bilingual education and multilingual fluency than ever before. The major problem for bilingual education, many of these educators believed, was not political but professional. The major problem was not how to restrain the opposition but how to find enough teachers for the growing number of students who qualified for bilingual education.[4]

The optimism of NABE bore fruit in the 1994 reauthorization of the Bilingual Education Act. Among many of the changes made, the proponents were able to strengthen the basis for federally supported bilingual education program implementation and to expand the goals of bilingual education to include not only the learning of English but also proficiency in more than one language and in multicultural understanding.[5] The opponents appeared to have lost significant ground in the reauthorization of the bilingual education act under President Clinton.[6]

While opposition to bilingual education decreased within the federal government, it continued in muted forms throughout the country. The vast majority of bilingual education opponents argued that this policy failed to teach immigrant children English.[7] Majority Whip Tom DeLay's rationale for introducing a bill to eliminate federal bilingual education policy in 1998 illustrated this widespread belief in the ineffectiveness of this program. Bilingual education programs, argued John Phillipe, DeLay's spokesperson, "have failed to live up to their promise" of making it easier for children to learn English. "When you have bilingual education programs," he added, "you are telling [immigrant children] that they don't need to learn English to get by."[8]

Other opponents questioned the pluralist goals of bilingual education and the role of the federal government in prescribing bilingual education-only approaches. Rosalie Pedalino Porter, for instance, argued that bilingual education was not working in assimilating ELLs into American life.[9] Although good in theory, she noted in 1990, bilingual education was fostering and prolonging ethnic segregation, robbing children of their chance to become full participants in American life, and contributing to the fragmentation of this nation into competing ethnic groups.

The notion of fragmentation in American life and the failure to teach assimilation were reflected in other popular books by well-known individuals such as Arthur M. Schlesinger, Jr., and William J. Bennett. Schlesinger decried multiculturalism that, in his opinion, resulted in the "disuniting of America," threatening its social fabric and core values. Bennett charged that a "cultural elite" of academics and liberal policymakers "devalued" America. He called for a "cultural war" to return to traditional values.[10]

During the second half of the 1990s, the attacks against bilingual education became increasingly strident. The reauthorization of the 1994 Bilingual Education Act, the 1996 presidential election and the anti-bilingual initiatives in California and Arizona, among other factors, were extremely important in creating a context for increased opposition to bilingual education at the national level.

The upsurge in opposition to bilingual education began shortly after the reauthorization of Title VII. This policy came under fierce attack on Capitol Hill and in the press. The 104th Congress considered legislation to repeal the law, to eliminate funding, and to outlaw most federal government operations in other languages.[11]

Opposition to bilingual education also increased in 1995 when Sen. Bob Dole, in his quest for the presidency, spoke before an American Legion national convention in Indianapolis against bilingual education and for making English the official language of the country. He warned his audience that "ethnic separatism" was a threat to American unity and called for making English the official language of the country.[12]

The syndicated columnist Joan Beck supported Dole's criticism of bilingual education and his argument in favor of an English-only policy. Similar to Dole, she argued that bilingual education had overly emphasized multiculturalism and diversity. These goals, she further noted, were having a detrimental impact on American society because they were leading to language segregation and ethnic separatism.[13] Bilingual education, in other words, was fostering the "balkanization" or fragmentation of American society.[14]

In the next several years, countless articles opposed to bilingual education appeared. Most of them were critical of this program because it allegedly promoted multiculturalism at the expense of Americanism, it did not teach immigrant children English, and because Latino parents opposed it.[15]

Popular opinion likewise became increasingly hostile towards bilingual education in the latter part of the 1990s. In Texas, the favorable attitude towards native language instruction in the public schools reported by NABE members in the early 1990s had soured. According to one poll, approximately fifty-two percent of several hundred Texans interviewed by telephone in May 1998 were opposed to bilingual education programs in the schools or else supported it for one year only. Forty-eight percent said "long-term" bilingual education should be eliminated because it "slows children's transition to mainstream American life and because they can easily learn a new language."[16] In California, voters decided in June 1998 to abandon bilingual education in favor of one-year English immersion classes. Voters in Arizona soon followed California's lead and mandated English-only instruction in their public schools.[17] In 2001–2002, several additional states introduced anti-bilingual or English-only initiatives in their legislative sessions: Colorado, Massachusetts, New York, Oklahoma, Oregon, and Iowa. Public opinion indeed appeared to be against bilingual education during the latter part of the 1990s regardless of who was behind these initiatives or the degree of bias found in the popular media.[18]

Scholarly articles opposed to bilingual education and in support of English-only methods likewise surfaced. One of these studies, for instance, interpreted the findings of a National Research Council report to mean that, despite a generation of research, "there is no evidence that there will be long-term advantages or disadvantages to teaching limited-English students in the native language."[19] Another study continued to show that bilingual education simply did not work.[20]

Supporters of bilingual education responded to these strident attacks in the latter part of the 1990s. They noted that the arguments against bilingual education were "bogus," that no significant research showing the success of English-only methods existed, and that findings showing the success of well-designed bilingual programs were distorted or suppressed.[21] Some of them even argued that to defeat the opponents of bilingual education, the supporters had to do a better job of educating the public about the successes and benefits of bilingual education. "Without a serious, dedicated and organized campaign to explain and defend bilingual education at the national level," argued Steve Krashen, "in a very short time we will have nothing left to defend."[22]

CHANGES IN POLICY

As in the prior decade, the opponents of bilingual education also sought legislative changes to this policy. Between 1995 and 2001, several pieces of legislation aimed at eliminating or modifying the federal bilingual education bill were introduced.

One of the most publicized efforts to eliminate bilingual education was submitted by House Majority Whip Tom DeLay, R-TX. In March and April of 1998 DeLay drafted and introduced legislation that would have removed the federal mandate on bilingual education by abolishing the Education Department's Office of Bilingual Education and effectively ended federal involvement in this program. This legislation, English for Children Act, was modeled after the proposition to be voted upon by California voters in the general election in November of 1998. If enacted, it would have voided the consent decrees that encouraged the establishment of bilingual programs in return for federal funding. More specifically, it would have effectively ended federal funding for about 750 bilingual programs nationwide that allowed the teaching of immigrant children in their native language until they learned English. It also would have saved the government an estimated $215 million a year. Once these decrees were voided, state and local school officials would decide for themselves whether they wanted to continue funding bilingual education programs.[23] LULAC as well as Gene Green and Sheila Jackson, both members of Congress from the Houston area, denounced DeLay's bill.[24]

Legislation such as DeLay's aimed at repealing bilingual education had been tried for years without much success. More successful were those aimed at modifying bilingual legislation. During the years from 1998 to 2001 several attempts were made to change bilingual education policy. The opposition forces succeeded in 2001.

The efforts to modify bilingual education resurfaced in the early months of the 1998 congressional session. In September of this year, the House approved HR 3892: the English Language Fluency Act. The Senate, however, did not approve the measure since Congress adjourned a month after its passage. If enacted, HR 3892 would have converted funding for bilingual and immigrant education programs to a block grant, placed a limit of three years on bilingual education, nullified all compliance agreements related to bilingual education between states or districts and the Department of Education, and changed the name of the Education Department's Office of Bilingual and Minority-languages Affairs to the Office of English-Language Acquisition.[25]

In May of the following year, President Clinton and Secretary of Education Riley submitted a new bill aimed at reauthorizing both the bilingual education act as well as the larger Elementary and Secondary Education Act. This education bill was to expire on September 30, 1999. The proposed legislation, the Educational Excellence for All Children Act of 1999, addressed the issues of bilingual education for ELLs within the context of this larger bill.[26]

In early July 1999, the U.S. House of Representatives Subcommittee on Early Childhood, Youth and Families, which is within the House Education and Workforce Committee, held the only field hearing on the reauthorization of the ESEA and bilingual education, in McAllen, Texas. The presenters, all supporters of bilingual education, in general noted that this policy had come under fire because of misconceptions, double standards and an ignorance of research that proved its effectiveness. More specifically, they made several arguments. First, they argued that language minority children needed to be viewed as assets, not deficits. Instead of LEP, they proposed the new term English language learners (ELLs). Since then, most supporters have tended to use this term to refer to those students needing bilingual education services. Most opponents, however, continue to use the term LEP in reference to these children. Second, they criticized placing emphasis on English language learning at the expense of academic learning and imposing time limits on students enrolled in bilingual programs. Third, they argued that bilingual education was emotionally charged and needed to be depoliticized, but no specific recommendations were made on how to do this.[27]

The House Committee on Education and Workforce approved the Elementary and Secondary Education Act in mid-October 1999. Although it was a bipartisan compromise, it included a very harmful provision on "parental notification and consent for English Language Learners." This provision, argued NABE and numerous educational and civil rights organizations opposed to it, would result in denying access for millions of ELL students to important Title I educational services.

At this date the Title VII bill had not yet been drafted. It was still being negotiated with the committee staff. Several areas of concern, however, had emerged by then. One of these was that the committee was planning on converting bilingual education into a formula grant program. Another one was that the Republicans on the committee wanted to stress programs that used English-only to teach English as well as discourage or prohibit using "native language instruction" in bilingual education. Finally, the committee was considering scaling back professional development activities, ensuring program accountability by limiting funding to three years, and eliminating the National Clearinghouse for Bilingual Education.[28]

In November, the reauthorization of the ESEA failed to go any further because of pre-election posturing by members of Congress and by bitter partisanship.[29]

In 2001, George W. Bush, a Republican, assumed the presidency. Republicans also gained influence in the Senate and House and for one year controlled both chambers. The Senate reverted to the Democrats the following year because of a defection of one senator from the Republican Party. These political developments significantly influenced the shaping of the new bilingual education bill.[30]

From the beginning of his administration, President Bush expressed his support for eliminating the federal preference for bilingual education and for supporting English-only methods for teaching ELLs. President Bush and the Republican Party also supported placing a three-year limit on bilingual education, setting performance objectives to ensure that these children achieve English fluency within these three years, and converting bilingual education from discretionary to block grants. President Bush's education plan likewise called for states to be held accountable for making annual increases in English proficiency from the previous year and for them to ensure that ELLs met standards in core content areas that were at least as rigorous as those in classes taught in English.[31]

Sometime in the spring, legislators in both chambers introduced their own versions of the reauthorization of the ESEA and of the Bilingual Education Act. The Senate and House passed S.1 and H.R. 1, respectively, in the spring. Despite the passage of these bills, many on Capitol Hill, as well as President Bush, were not certain that either of them could be enacted in 2001. Neither bill was workable, noted David S. Broder, a Washington columnist.[32]

In early August 2001, a committee was formed by Congress to work out the differences between the House and Senate versions of the legislation and to issue a final Conference Report. No Latinos or Latinas were appointed to this committee.[33]

Partisanship and inertia by early September, however, held up final work on the bill. "The partisan atmosphere on Capitol Hill was awful," noted Sandy Kress, a White House aide. The terrorist attack on America as well as the political upheaval transferring political control of the Senate to the Democrats however served as catalysts for education reform. The attack in particular encouraged the conference leaders to move forward to "demonstrate to the country that Congress had not been immobilized," said Margaret Spellings, another White House aide. The change in political control of the Senate made Edward M. Kennedy, a "consummate professional" with a "great staff," the new chairperson of the education reform effort in that chamber. President Bush showed his willingness to work with Kennedy to pass his education bill and Kennedy, in turn, said that he "saw a real opportunity for common ground."[34]

With these new political factors in place, the Committee completed its work in late September and issued its report, which then went to a floor vote in each chamber.[35]

The Senate approved the education reform bill (87–10) during the first week in December; the House approved it on Thursday, December 13, 2001, on a vote of 381–41. This bill authorized $26.5 billion in federal spending for the 2002 fiscal year that began October 1, a roughly $7 billion increase over 2001. It set up a comprehensive testing system to identity failing schools and needy students. It also stipulated that failing schools would receive resources to get them back on track, and that students could be offered the option of transferring to another public school or could get tutoring or other supplemental services.[36]

On January 8, 2002, President Bush signed the No Child Left Behind Act of 2001 (H.R. 1) into law.[37] This legislation amended and reauthorized the ESEA for the next six years. It also reauthorized the BEA of 1994. The former bilingual education act, known as Title VII of the ESEA, is now Title III of the No Child Left Behind Act. Its official title is "Language Instruction for Limited English Proficient and Immigrant Children."

THE REPEAL OF BILINGUAL EDUCATION, 2001

Title III represents a major overhaul of federal programs for the education of English Language Learners, or as the Bush administration calls them, limited English proficient and recent immigrant students. More particularly, it officially repeals bilingual education and replaces it with an English-only piece of legislation.

The bill has a short authorization section and three major subparts. Parts A and B are different components of the education act and the core of the bill. Part C focuses on definitions of key terms mentioned in the bill.

Part A is quite distinct from Part B. The goals of both Parts A and B share some similarities. Both, for instance, promote English fluency among ELLs and encourage meeting the challenging academic and achievement standards throughout the country. Despite these surface similarities, there are some major differences. Part A for instance, promotes only English fluency whereas Part B promotes multilingual fluency and multicultural understanding. Part A also promotes academic achievement in English only whereas Part B promotes academic achievement in English plus.

TABLE 1

GOALS IN PARTS A AND B OF TITLE III
(FORMALLY THE BILINGUAL EDUCATION ACT), 2001

PART A	PART B
TITLE—English Language Acquisition, Language Enhancement, and Academic Achievement Act	**TITLE**—Improving Language Instruction Educational Programs for Academic Achievement Act.
PURPOSES	**PURPOSES**
Establishes a program for both LEP & Immigrant children.	Maintains distinct programs for LEP and Immigrant Children.
Promotes English-only instructional programs.	Maintains bilingual instructional programs.
Promotes monolingualism and monoculturalism.	Promotes multilingual proficiency and multicultural understanding.
Helps LEP/immigrant children meet high levels of academic achievement in English only.	Helps LEP children meet rigorous academic achievement standards in English plus.
Holds SEAs, LEAs and schools accountable for increased in English proficiency and in core academic content knowledge of LEP children by requiring demonstrated improvement in English.	Promotes systemic improvement and reform of educational programs servicing LEP children.
Provide SEAs and LEAs with flexibility in implementing LIEP based on scientifically based research on teaching LEP children English.	Develops data collection and dissemination, research materials, and technical assistance that are focused on school improvement for LEP children.

The major provisions of each part also differ substantially. Part A establishes a formula grant program for developing English-only instructional programs whereas Part B maintains a competitive grant program for the establishment and enhancement of bilingual programs. Both hold state and local educational agencies accountable for increases in English proficiency and in core academic content and encourage the funding of professional development activities. Part B, however, authorizes the secretary of education to conduct data collection, dissemination, and research on ELLs and on bilingual education and to encourage the development and dissemination of instructional materials for bilingual programs. Part A does not.

TABLE 2

PROVISIONS OF PARTS A AND B OF TITLE III (FORMALLY THE BILINGUAL EDUCATION ACT), 2001

PART A	PART B
OTHER PROVISIONS	OTHER PROVISIONS
Establishes a formula grant program for establishing English only instructional programs.	Maintains a competitive grant program for the establishment and enhancement of bilingual programs.
Establishes an accountability system based on two year evaluations focusing on teaching English and meeting academic and achievement standards.	Establishes an accountability system based on two year evaluations of bilingual programs and on professional development activities.
Is silent on the need to support data collection, dissemination, and research on LEP children and on instructional programs for them.	Authorizes Secretary to conduct data collection, dissemination, and research on LEP children and on bilingual education.
Ignores the development and dissemination of instructional materials for bilingual programs.	Encourages the development and dissemination of Instructional Materials for bilingual programs.
Encourages the funding of professional development activities (SUBPART 3).	Encourages the funding of professional development activities.

PART A continued	PART B continued
OTHER PROVISIONS	OTHER PROVISIONS
No special funding is provided for immigrant children.	Provides funds for establishing special programs and services to educate immigrant children.
The Secretary shall neither mandate nor preclude the use of a particular curricular or pedagogical approach to educating LEP children.	
The Secretary shall coordinate and ensure close cooperation with all entities serving LEP children.	

In summary, Part A promotes a formula-based block grant to the states for establishing English-only programs, whereas Part B maintains a competitive grant program for the establishment and strengthening of bilingual education. According to the bill, only one of these parts can be in effect at any particular time. Part A can be in effect if the amount appropriated by Congress equals or exceeds $650 million dollars. Part B can be in effect only if Part A is not. Which part is in effect then depends on the amount of money appropriated by Congress.[38]

On January 2002, Congress appropriated $665 million dollars for FY2002.[39] Based on this appropriation, only Part A would be in effect. The large appropriation thus means that, for all intents and purposes, bilingual education has been repealed and replaced by an English-only bill for ELLs and immigrant children.

Title III, in essence, reverses the language policy enacted in 1994. This policy promoted academic achievement, multilingual proficiency, and multicultural understanding. It also encouraged capacity-building and provided substantial funds for teacher training, research, and support services. Title III stresses academic achievement and the learning of English only. The rapid teaching of English, notes James Crawford, will take precedence over everything else. "Accountability provisions, such as judging schools by the percentage of English Language Learners reclassified as fluent in English each year, are expected to discourage the use of native-language instruction," he stated. "Annual English assessments will be mandated, 'measurable achievement objectives' will be established, and failure to show academic progress in English will be punished," he further adds.[40]

Title III likewise limits funding for capacity-building activities and restricts it to 6.5 percent of the total budget or about $43 million for fiscal year 2002. The year before, funding for these types of activities amounted to $100 million. The limited funding in Title III will do little to address the critical shortage of teachers qualified to meet the needs of ELLs.[41]

Strangely enough, the radical change in policy occurred without any major opposition from the proponents of bilingual education. Although groups such as NABE, LULAC, and the National Council de La Raza had opposed many of the provisions included in Title III, neither liberal Democrats or members of the Congressional Hispanic Caucus "voted against the legislation at any stage of the process or sponsored a single amendment to preserve the federal bilingual education program." Prominent members of Congress and former allies of Title VII, such as Edward Kennedy, likewise failed to defend native-language programs and willingly accepted the changes demanded by Republicans in order to pass Bush's education bill.[42]

More significantly, traditional allies of Title VII have failed to provide an honest assessment of this new bill. No major statements have been issued by groups such as NABE, MALDEF, or LULAC on this bill. The only exceptions to this "silence" by the supporters of bilingual education are James Crawford, the noted journalist, and Raul Izaguirre, director of the National Council de la Raza.

Crawford, in an obituary for the Bilingual Education Act, argued that Title VII "expired" quietly on January 8. The death of the thirty-four-year-old law, he notes "was not unexpected, following years of attacks by enemies and recent desertions by allies in Congress." He further notes that while federal funds will continue to support the education of ELLs, the money will be spent to support programs aimed at developing English only. The repeal of bilingual education in general and the expunging of the word bilingual and the goal of proficiency in two languages, in particular, he added, "happened with barely a peep from the traditional political allies of bilingual education."[43]

Izaguirre, on the other hand, writes more favorably of Title III and of the larger ESEA. Although he is silent on the elimination of native language instruction in Title III and on the replacement of the Bilingual Education Act with an English-only measure, he makes several points in his analysis of this bill. First, Izaguirre commends the Conference Committee considering the reauthorization of the ESEA for completing work in this bill and for engaging in "a careful, deliberative process." During this process, he notes, "members of Congress displayed a degree of statesmanship that, compared to the demagoguery that has characterized the debate over bilingual education in California, Arizona, and Massachusetts, eschewed political rhetoric and maintained a focus on truly helping ELL students achieve academically while mastering English."[44] No mention is made of the exclusion of Latinos from the Conference Committee or of the role Kennedy and other Democrats played in abandoning the interests of bilingual education advocates. Second, he praises some key provisions and fails to criticize them or only provides moderate criticism of their potential negative impact on Latino students. He, for instance, praises the provisions to improve teachers' skills, provide parents with the information and options they need to choose the right instructional program for children, and hold schools more accountable for helping ELLs acquire English and meet challenging academic benchmarks. But he fails to point out that, at least with respect to Title III, the new legislation significantly cuts back funds for professional development and for supportive services aimed at helping ELLs acquire English and meet challenging academic content. He also supports the block grant awards and the increases in federal funds to all states that have ELL students, "not just the school districts that apply for grants through a competitive process." This support, however, was not without reservations.

Given that state governments are likely to experience budget deficits over the next several years while the number of ELLs continues to grow we approach this shift in policy with caution. Unless the schools receive increased resources to serve these additional ELLs, then the funds could end up being spread too thinly among schools to be effective. Thus, we believe that proper implementation of this legislation means that the Congress and the Bush Administration must close the loop by providing states the resources and technical assistance they need to provide ELLs with a quality education. In addition, they must more effectively monitor implementation of the program to ensure that the states are able to meet the ambitious goal.[45]

CONCLUSION

The passage of this bill means that after several decades of attacking and undermining this policy the opponents have finally succeeded in repealing bilingual education and in replacing it with an English-only one. The forces of conservatism, assimilation, and ignorance, in other words, have triumphed over pluralism and over enlightened pedagogy. Is this, then, the beginning of the end for bilingualism in the United States or is this only a temporary setback? Nobody really knows at this point. But if history is any guide, we are bound to see the clash between contending groups with competing notions of assimilation, ethnicity, empowerment, social change, and pedagogy continue and probably escalate in the years ahead. Contestation and contradiction have and will continue to shape the content of school language policies in the years to come for they are central to the policy development process. It might be appropriate here to end this history with the words of Josué M. González, one of the most important and influential advocates of bilingual education in the nation. Recently, in reflecting on the demise of federal bilingual education policy and on the federal government's support for this policy, he noted that this temporary setback will not have a dampening effect on bilingualism or on dual language instruction. In the wake of this demise, González stated, bilingual educators throughout the country are building new and more exciting programs for all children. He added:

Better and more potent forms of bilingual teaching have begun to emerge. Most of these are no longer transitional, remedial, or compensatory. The new bilingual education programs of the 21st century will have new dreams and new keywords that reflect the new and more powerful dreams of a diverse nation: biliteracy, enrichment, two-way, language for global understanding, and heritage language preservation.[46]

The contestation embedded in policymaking, in other words, will continue to exist into the new century. In more particular language, the battle for federal bilingual education policy has ended with the passage of the No Child Left Behind Act, but the larger war for bilingualism and dual language instruction is yet to be won.

NOTES

1. Nancy Mathis, "Study Lauds Bilingual Education," *Houston Chronicle*, 12 February 1991, 1A.
2. Mathis, "Study Lauds."
3. Mathis, "Study Lauds."
4. William Pack, "Future Appears Secure for Bilingual Education," *Houston Post*, 27 February 1993, 13H.
5. For a summary of the research used to strengthen federal support for bilingual education in the 1994 reauthorization process see James Crawford, *Best Evidence: Research Foundations of the Bilingual Education Act* (Washington, D.C.: National Clearinghouse for Bilingual Education, 1997).
6. Bilingual Education Act of 1994, *Public Law 103–382*, September 28, 1994, Part A, Sec.7102 (a)(14); Sec. 7102(b); and 7102(c).
7. See, for instance, Jorge Amselle, "'Texas' Bilingual Mandates Are a Disservice to All," *Houston Chronicle*, 24 March 1997, 19A; and Douglas Lasken, "Best Way to Teach Students English? End Bilingual Education," *Houston Chronicle*, 19 January 1998, 19A.
8. Greg McDonald, "DeLay to Target Bilingual Classes/Bill Would Eliminate Federal Office, Funds," *Houston Chronicle*, 22 April 1998, 1A.

9. Rosalie Pedalino Porter, *Forked Tongue: The Politics of Bilingual Education* (New York: Basic Books, 1990).

10. Arthur M. Schlesinger, Jr., *The Disuniting of America* (New York: W.W. Norton, 1992); and William J. Bennett, *The Devaluing of America: The Fight for Our Culture and Our Children* (New York: Touchstone, 1992).

11. Crawford, *Best Evidence*, 1.

12. For a summary of his talk see David S. Broder, "Dole Gives Support to Making English the Official Language," *Houston Chronicle*, 5 September 1995, 2A.

13. Joan Beck, "Emphasize What Unites U.S.—English," *Houston Chronicle*, 12 September 1995, 16A; and "English-Only Law Would Make a Better America," *Houston Chronicle*, 9 March 1997, 3C.

14. On more general ideological attacks on immigrants who spoke these different languages see Peter Brimelow, *Alien Nation: Common Sense About America's Immigration Disaster* (New York: Harper Perennial, 1996). He argues that the U.S. was in danger of becoming an "alien nation" overrun by immigrants from Asia and Latin America who inflict a "demographic mutation" on the national character of the country. He feared that Latinos had emerged as a "strange anti-nation in the U.S." and embodied the "American anti-ideal" by their refusal to Americanize and be absorbed as Americans.

15. See, for instance, Lasken, "Best Way;" and Amselle, "Texas' Bilingual Mandates;" and Alan Bernstein, "Bilingual Debate has Texas Twang/Most Texans Oppose Method that Takes Years," *Houston Chronicle*, 25 May 1998, 1A.

16. Bernstein, "Texas Twang."

17. James Crawford, "Bilingual Education: Strike Two," *Rethinking Schools* 15:2 (Winter 2000–2001): 1.

18. *Issues in U.S. Language Policy: Language Legislation in the U.S.A.*, n.d., James Crawford Website: http://ourworld.compuserve.com/homepages/jwcrawford/Langleg.htm.

19. Charles L. Glenn, *What Does the National Research Council Study Tell Us About Educating Language Minority Children?* (Amherst, MA: READ Institute, 1997). The supporters of bilingual education vigorously rejected this interpretation. They argued that "empirical results . . . support the theory underlying native language instruction." See Diane August and Kenji Hakuta, Letter to Rosalie Porter, READ Institute. Cited in James Crawford, "Bilingual Education," James Crawford Website, cited above.

20. See, for instance, C. Rossell and R. Baker, "The Educational Effectiveness of Bilingual Education," *Research in the Teaching of English* 30:1 (1996): 7–74 .

21. James Crawford, *At War with Diversity: U.S. Language Policy in an Age of Anxiety* (Buffalo, NY: Multilingual Matters, 2000); Stephen D. Krashen, *Under Attack: The Case Against Bilingual Education* (Culver City, CA: Language Education Associates, 1996); Stephen D. Krashen, *Condemned Without a Trial: Bogus Arguments Against Bilingual Education* (Westport, CT: Heinemann, 1999); James Crawford, "Ten Common Fallacies About Bilingual Education," *ERIC Digest,* November 1998, EDO-FL-98–10 (available through James Crawford's Language Policy Web Site cited above); Jay Greene, *A Meta-Analysis of the Effectiveness of Bilingual Education* (Claremont, CA: Tomás Rivera Center, 1998).

22. Stephen Krashen, "Evidence Suggesting That Public Opinion is Becoming More Negative: A Discussion of the Reasons, and What We Can Do About It," n.d., p. 4. *http://ourworld.compuserve.com/homepages/JWCRAWFORD/Krash11.htm.* See also "Bilingual Education: A Goal for All Children," *Rethinking Schools Online* 15:2 (Winter 2000/2001): 1–3. *http://www.rethinkingschools.org/Archives/15_02/Edit152.htm.*

23. For information on DeLay's bill see the following: Greg McDonald, "DeLay May Press to Let States End Bilingual Education/Bill Would Abolish Federal Mandate," *Houston Chronicle,* 25 March 1998, 2A; McDonald, "DeLay to Target." For a statement in support of DeLay's bill, see Eric J. Stone, Director of Research, U.S. English, "Testimony Before the House Subcommittee on Early Childhood, Youth and Families, regarding H.R. 3892, The English Language Fluency Act," 30 April 1998. Found in *www.us-english.org/betestimony.htm.*

24. Jo Ann Zuniga, Greg McDonald, staff, "DeLay's Bill Attacking Bilingual Education Gathering Opposition," *Houston Chronicle,* 25 April 1998, 35A.

25. For information on this bill see Joetta L. Sack, "Bilingual Education Legislation Passes House," *Teacher Magazine on the Web,* 16 September 1998, 1, *http://www.teachermagazine.org/ew/vol-18/02biling.h18.*

26. For a brief view of this bill see "Proposed ESEA Reauthorization and Title VII, *National Clearinghouse on Bilingual Education Newsline,* 29 May 1999, *http://www.ncbe.gwu.edu/newsline/1999/05/28.htm.* Online text, summaries and analysis of the Educational Excellence for All Children Act of 1999 can be found through the Department of Education web site: *http://www.ed.gov/offices/OESE/ESEA.*

27. For information on the presenters and the arguments made in this hearing see Allie Johnson, "Texas Educators Lobby to Reauthorize Bilingual Education," *The McAllen*

Monitor, 8 July 1999. N.p.; Cecilia Balli, "Educators Push for Bilingual Education," *San Antonio Express-News,* no date, (both articles found in "Bilingual education file," Local History Room, La Retama Library, Corpus Christi, Texas.)

28. For comments on these actions, on the proposed changes in bilingual education, and on the recommended responses by the supporters of this program see "NABE Action Alert: Title VII Reauthorization bill moves through house committee," E-mail from Michele Hewlett-Gomez to supporters of bilingual education, Sun, October 3, 1999, pp. 1–3, and "NABE Action Alert: Update on Federal Legislation Impacting Language-Minority Children," E-mail from Michele Hewlett-Gomez to supporters of bilingual education, Sunday, October 17, 1999. (both of these are in author's possession.)

29. David S. Broder, "How the Education Bill Was Born," *The Washington Post National Weekly,* 24 December 2001–6 January 2002, 14–15.

30. Broder, "How the Education Bill," 15.

31. For Bush's proposals on bilingual education in particular and education in general see Erik W. Robelen, "Bush Plan: No Child Will Be Left Behind—Democrats, GOP Agree in Principle on Federal Role," *Education Week,* 31 January 2001, 1, 24. For a view of these proposed changes see Mary Ann Zehr, "Bush Plan Could Alter Bilingual Education," *Education Week on the Web,* 21 February 2001, 1–6. *www.edweek.org/ ew/ewstory.cfm?slug=23biling.h20.*

32. Broder, "How the Education Bill," 15.

33. For a list of the conferees see *NABE Action Alert: Congress Appoints Conferees on Legislation Governing Federal Bilingual Education,* 2 August 2001, 1–7 (in author's possession).

34. Broder, "How the Education Bill," 14.

35. For a view of NABE's views on this legislation in early August see *NABE Action Alert.* For a copy of this bill see *No Child Left Behind, Title III,* 3 August 2001. pp. 270–315. *www.ed.gov/inits/nclb/part7.html.*

36. See "House OKs School Reform Bill," *Houston Chronicle,* 14 December 2001, 10A.

37. *Public Law 107–110,* (Jan 8, 2002). For an analysis of its provisions see House of Representatives, *No Child Left Behind Act of 2001, Conference Report to Accompany H.R. 1,* 107th Congress, 1st Sess., Report 107–334, December 13, 2001, Sec. 3001.

38. See House of Representatives, *No Child Left Behind Act of 2001.*

39. Jeffrey J. Kuenzi, *Education of Limited English Proficient and Recent Immigrant Students: Provisions in the No Child Left Behind Act of 2001, March 1, 2002* (Washington, D.C.: Congressional Research Service, the Library of Congress, March 1, 2002), 1.

40. James Crawford, *Obituary: The Bilingual Education Act, 1968–2002,* Spring 2002, 1. *http://ourworld.compuserve.com/homepages/jwcrawford/T7obit.htm.*

41. James Crawford, *Obituary,* 1.

42. James Crawford, *Obituary,* 2. For another view of how liberal Democrats agreed to work with Republicans to pass the ESEA see Broder, "How the Education Bill."

43. James Crawford, *Obituary,* 1–2.

44. *Statement of Raul Yzaguirre on the Elementary and Secondary Education Act,* 14 December 2001, 1. NCLR Website. (In author's possession). See *www.nclr.org.*

45. *Statement of Raul Yzaguirre.*

46. Josué M. González, "Editor's Introduction: Bilingual Education and the Federal Role, If Any . . . ," *Bilingual Research Journal* 26:2 (Summer 2002): ix.

CONCLUSION

INTRODUCTION

This brief history focused on one of the most contentious and misunderstood policies in the country: federal bilingual education. It traced and explained, in bold sketches, the rise and fall of federal bilingual education policy during the years from 1960 to 2001 and the role played by the contending groups of supporters and opponents in its development.

Three major findings were presented in this book. First, this study showed that contestation, conflict, and accommodation were integral aspects of federal bilingual education policy development. From its origins in the 1960s to the present, different groups with competing notions of ethnicity, assimilation, pedagogy, and power have contended, clashed, struggled, and negotiated with each other for hegemony in the development and implementation of bilingual education. Second, contextual forces over time, especially electoral politics and a changing political climate at the national, state, and local level, significantly shaped the contours and content of this policy. Finally, those supportive of or opposed to federal bilingual education displayed a wide array of political, educational, and social reasons for their actions.

CONTESTATION AND FEDERAL BILINGUAL EDUCATION POLICY

Contestation, conflict, and accommodation became apparent in the 1960s when language specialists, professional educators, non-white language minorities, and minority civil rights advocates led the struggle for the enactment of the first Bilingual Education Act in this country. These groups fought against opposition within the federal government and against the passive resistance of many individuals and groups who misunderstood or were ignorant of the merits of native language instruction.

Origins

As a group, these activists rejected subtractive schooling, exclusionary educational policies, and limited reform. They also took advantage of the new social and political climate in the society and articulated oppositional or alternative ideologies and structures aimed at supporting pluralism, political empowerment, and significant educational change.

Most of these educators and activists, for practical purposes, focused on language as the linchpin of significant school reform. Specific language reforms were proposed by activists including the repeal of English-only laws and the enactment of federal and state bilingual education legislation.

Despite their efforts, the heterogeneous group of bilingual education supporters only managed to enact a minor piece of legislation. The bill—the Bilingual Education Act of 1968—was programmatically small and both categorical in nature and compensatory in intent. Also, the policy's purpose and the program's goals were vague or undefined. During the next decade or so, they took it upon themselves to transform this minor voluntary piece of legislation aimed at low-income, "limited-English-speaking" students into a major reform aimed at all children.

Expansion: Changed Character

The contestation embedded in policy making continued in muted forms during the first decade of its implementation. Despite pervasive passive resistance or non-support for bilingual education, the proponents made several important changes to this policy.

First, they transformed the voluntary character of federal bilingual education policy and made it mandatory. Increased federal involvement became important in this effort.[1] Second, they eliminated the experimental approach to educating language minority children and established a federal preference for using native language instructional approaches.[2] Third, they delineated the goals of federal bilingual education policy and tried to expand them from meeting the academic needs of poor language minority children to promoting bilingualism and biculturalism in all the public schools. Fourth, they tried to turn bilingual education policy into an enrichment program serving all children regardless of socioeconomic status or language ability.[3] Finally, they increased the bill's funding and expanded its scope to include capacity building activities. The policy, in other words, expanded to include not only the funding of bilingual educational instructional programs for language minority students but also professional development, curriculum development, research and data collection, and federal administration. With respect to the latter, for instance, the proponents of this policy encouraged the federal government to establish a national office of bilingual education, a national advisory group of bilingual education, and a national clearinghouse on bilingual education.[4]

Emergence of Opposition

These changes in bilingual education policy, in addition to other factors such as the growth of bilingualism in American institutional life, the structural inclusion of ethnic minorities, the continuing waves of immigration, the growing presence and influence of non-English-speaking groups on American culture, and the swings in the economy, created fears and anxieties among Americans of all colors, classes, and genders. These developments, in turn, sparked a vigorous opposition to bilingual education policy among federal policymakers, local school officials, administrators, and lay persons. In the latter part of the 1970s, this opposition was highly disorganized and limited primarily to journalists and researchers. In the 1980s and 1990s, Republican officeholders in the executive and legislative branch of the federal government and special interest groups, especially English-only organizations, conservative educators, and parent groups joined the battle against bilingual education.

The opponents pursued two major strategies. Both of them were highly contested by the proponents. One of these was aimed at attacking the empirical basis of bilingual education, the other one at repealing or modifying federal bilingual education policy.

Attacking Bilingual Education

The first major strategy raised questions about the goals, effectiveness, and consequences of federal bilingual education. From the beginning emphasis was placed on questioning its effectiveness. During the 1970s, opponents began to argue that bilingual education was not effective in teaching ELLs English or in improving their academic achievement.[5] During the following decade, they introduced the notion that alternatives to bilingual education existed.[6] Among the ones most commonly mentioned were English immersion and English as a Second Language approaches.[7]

Other critics argued that bilingual education was not assimilating immigrant children as fast as it could, that it was promoting Hispanic separatism and cultural apartheid, that it was an affirmative action program for Latinos, or that the federal government was "dictating" the curriculum at the local level by mandating one single approach to educating ELLs.[8]

Opponents likewise developed a variety of novel arguments against bilingual education in the 1980s and 1990s. Some of these were in specific reference to bilingual education itself and to the issues surrounding the program. Among some of the most important arguments of this type were that non-linguistic factors were responsible for the lower achievement of many language minority students, that local educational agencies had severe financial, personnel, and assessment constraints that inhibited their ability to provide services and that the size of the language minority population eligible for federal services was smaller than had been estimated in prior years and most of them were already being served by bilingual education programs.[9]

Other arguments were broader in nature and related to the role of the federal government, ideas of second language learning, public opinion, and the history of bilingual education in the U.S. Opponents, for instance, argued, among other things, that there was no federal legal requirement for schools to provide bilingual or bicultural education; that public opinion was against bilingual education; that language minority parents did not support bilingual education because they felt it was more important for their children to learn English than to maintain the native language; that English was losing ground to other languages in the United States; or that newcomers to the United States were learning English more slowly now than in previous generations.[10]

The proponents of bilingual education at some point in time countered all of these charges. A few of them criticized the methodological flaws and conclusions of studies indicating that bilingual education programs were not effectively teaching ELLs.[11] Some of them argued that no significant research showing the success of English-only methods existed and that findings showing the success of well-designed bilingual programs were distorted or suppressed.[12] Others still noted that the attack against this policy was ideologically inspired or that the arguments against bilingual education were "bogus."[13]

Undermining Policy and Practice

In addition to attacking various aspects of bilingual education policy, the opposition also sought changes in federal bilingual education policy, in its funding, and in the federal role. The supporters of bilingual education, in most cases, contested these actions.

Opposition within the federal government came primarily from elected officials in the executive and legislative branch of government. The former I refer to as executive opponents, the latter as congressional opponents.

Executive opponents, led by two Republican Presidents, sought to weaken federal support for bilingual education. President Ronald Reagan initiated the campaign against bilingual education in 1980.[14]

He initially tried to halt the growth of bilingual education by seeking rescissions and decreased funding.[15] In the 1986–1987 fiscal year, however, the funding level for the bilingual education act increased to $143 million. The need for Latino votes in the presidential elections and the wooing of Latino voters by the Republican Party led to this increase.[16]

During his second term, President Reagan developed a new initiative to undermine bilingual education policy. He appointed William J. Bennett, an avid opponent of bilingual education, to head the Department of

Education and to lead this initiative against it. Once in office, Bennett developed and implemented a coherent plan to redirect the program towards more English instruction.[17] First, he eliminated the mandatory provisions of bilingual education by dismantling its civil rights component. More specifically, he withdrew the proposed and actual federal guidelines for ensuring compliance with non-discrimination policies. He also persuaded the Department of Education to develop new regulations aimed at promoting local flexibility in bilingual program design and at eliminating the use of non-English language instruction in these programs.[18] Second, he downgraded the primary instrument for enforcing the *Lau* decision, the Office for Civil Rights, by drastically reducing its budget and staff.[19] Finally, he weakened the administration of bilingual education and tried to undo existing *Lau* agreements.[20]

Proponents of bilingual education, especially Latino groups, opposed all of these changes and criticized Bennett for his shortsightedness and the negative implications his strategy could have on language minority children.[21] Their opposition had no significant impact on Bennett's drive to undermine bilingual education.

Congressional opponents also took a variety of actions against bilingual education. Between 1980 and 2001, for instance, they introduced countless pieces of legislation aimed at repealing the federal bilingual education bill. In many cases, they also introduced English-only bills in an effort to eliminate bilingual education policies. None of them became law.

Unable to repeal bilingual education, congressional opponents sought changes in the policy. Two key changes were made. One of these placed limits on the number of years ELLs could participate in bilingual programs (two to three years), on the number of English-speaking children eligible to participate (from forty percent of total to none), and on the amount of non-English languages one could use in bilingual education (less than half a day; less than one hour per day).[22] The other major change focused on redefining bilingual education policy to allow for the inclusion of non-English language approaches. In 1984, for instance, the Bilingual Education Act was modified to include the development of an English-only instructional program known as Special Alternative Instructional Programs (SAIP).[23] Funding was guaranteed for SAIP but not for the others. During the next decade, guaranteed funding for SAIP increased from ten to twenty-five percent of total bilingual education funds. Despite this gradual increase, the opponents of bilingual education continued to seek more drastic changes.[24]

In the first half of the 1990s, the election of President Clinton to the White House, a Democrat and a strong supporter of bilingual education, temporarily halted the opposition's efforts. However, during the second half of the decade, and as a result of the control by Republicans of both chambers of Congress in 1996 and the election of Republican George W. Bush to the White House in 2000, congressional opponents renewed their attempts to change bilingual education policy. In 2001, they succeeded in enacting a new bill with most of the provisions that they had wanted for a decade. This legislation, the No Child Left Behind Act, amended and reauthorized the ESEA for the next six years.[25] It authorized $26.5 billion in federal spending for the 2002 fiscal year that began October 1, a roughly $7 billion increase over 2001. It set up a comprehensive testing system to identity failing schools and needy students and stipulated that failing schools would get resources to get them back on track.[26]

This bill also reauthorized the BEA of 1994. It became Title III of the overall bill.[27] This title, a major overhauled of federal programs for the education of ELLs and recent immigrant students, provided more funds for their education but it also officially repealed bilingual education and replaced it with an English-only piece of legislation.[28] This bill signaled the fall of bilingual education policy at the federal level. Although the proponents lost this particular battle, Josué González, a lifelong supporter of this program noted in 2002, that the war over bilingualism in American life was far from being over.[29]

CONTEXTUAL FORCES IN BILINGUAL EDUCATION

This history has also shown that larger contextual forces in American life influenced federal bilingual education policy. The liberal climate of the War on Poverty and the Civil Rights era as well as the emerging research on bilingualism and cultural pluralism of the early 1960s provided a favorable climate for the development of arguments in support of bilingual education. During these years, language specialists, committed educators, civil rights advocates, Chicano/a activists, and others took advantage of the new social and political climate in society to articulate oppositional or alternative ideologies and structures aimed at supporting pluralism, political empowerment, and educational change.

Rising conservatism, especially the election of Republicans to the executive and legislative branch of government, became crucial determinants of federal policy change. The origins of serious opposition to bilingual education began with the election of Ronald Reagan to the White House in 1980. His administration initiated a significant shift in the federal government's support for bilingual education.[30] More specifically, President Reagan and his allies halted the growth of bilingual education and significantly modified this policy and its implementation.

Other factors also assisted opponents in reversing bilingual education advances during the 1980s, including the loss of nerve by liberal politicians to fight for their own ideals, the restlessness of the lay public over minority rights, domestic and international economic conditions, rapid immigration, especially from Asia, Latin America, and the Caribbean, the fragmentation of the left and progressive organizations, and the formation of the U.S. English-only movement.[31]

During the 1990s, congressional and presidential elections again became instrumental in either halting or accelerating the attacks against bilingual education. In this decade, a Democrat, William Jefferson Clinton, became president of the United States. Unlike former Republican presidents, Clinton was a strong supporter of bilingual education. While in office he not only blunted the further dismantling of bilingual education but he also strengthened this legislation. By the latter part of the 1990s, however, organized opposition to bilingual education significantly increased throughout the country. The anti-bilingual initiatives in California and Arizona and the English-only movement, among other factors, were extremely important in creating a context for increased opposition to bilingual education at the national level. The election of Republicans to the White House and to both chambers of Congress in 2000 also became an important element in the repeal of federal bilingual education. From the beginning of his administration, President George W. Bush, elected to office in 2000, expressed his support for eliminating the federal preference for bilingual education and for supporting English-only methods for teaching LEP children. President Bush and the Republican Party also supported placing a three-year limit on bilingual education, setting performance objectives to ensure that ELLs achieve English fluency within these three years, and converting bilingual education from discretionary to block grants. President Bush's education plan likewise called for states to be held accountable for making annual increases in English proficiency from the previous year and for them to ensure that these students met standards in core content areas that were at least as rigorous as those in classes taught in English.[32]

These sets of circumstances eventually led to the formulation and enactment of S. 1, the comprehensive education reform bill proposed by the Bush administration and to the repeal of the Bilingual Education Act of 1994.[33]

REASONS FOR OPPOSING OR SUPPORTING BILINGUAL EDUCATION

Federal bilingual education was supported or opposed by a large number of groups and individuals with diverse backgrounds and competing views on pluralism, nationality, pedagogy, federalism, and ethnicity. For the most part, supporters of this policy were ideologically opposed to the assimilationist philosophy underlying the subtractive and conformist policies and practices in the schools, to the structural exclusion and institutional discrimination of minority groups, and to limited school reform. They viewed bilingual education as a means for supporting a variety of goals, including academic achievement, cultural and linguistic pluralism, ethnic minority political empowerment, and significant school change.

The opponents of bilingual education were ideologically supportive of assimilation, the limited participation of ethnic minorities in public policy, and compensatory school reforms, that is, reforms aimed specifically at targeted groups of individuals requiring special services. Many of them opposed bilingual education for different reasons. Some of them wanted to reverse the gains made by the supporters of bilingual education and halt the growth of bilingual education throughout the country. More specifically, they wanted to decrease or eliminate the use of non-English languages in public education and improve the academic achievement of low-income ELLs through the teaching of English only. Others wanted to eliminate the mandatory aspects of this policy and the federal preference for bilingual education. Others still wanted to promote Americanization instead of cultural pluralism in the schools and limit community involvement in education.

These individuals and groups did not formally organize and mount an assault against bilingual education until the late 1970s. During the next several decades, opponents of bilingual education coalesced around several key ideas that included ideological opposition to pluralism, to an "intrusive" federal role, to significant language-based school reform, and to primary language instruction in public education.

CONCLUSION

During the past three and a half decades bilingual education policies have changed significantly largely as a result of political dissatisfactions and struggles between contending groups with competing notions of assimilation, ethnicity, pedagogy, and power. Educators supported the enactment of bilingual education to solve the problems of underachievement, structural exclusion, assimilation, and relative political powerlessness among Mexican Americans and other language minority groups. Over the decades, bilingual educators encountered significant organized resistance to the use of non-English languages in the schools and to the use of schools as instruments of minority empowerment. Opponents to bilingual education organized in the 1980s and began to challenge the need for primary language instruction in public policy. The following decade, they managed to reverse the gains made by its supporters in earlier years. In 2001, the opponents gained the upper hand and succeeded in repealing the federal bilingual education act. The participation by all

of these groups has led to significant conflict in the formulation, enactment, and implementation of bilingual education policy at all levels of
government. Clashes between different groups with contending views,
however, will continue to shape the content of school language policies
in the years to come for contestation, conflict, and accommodation are
central to the policy development process.

NOTES

1. *Lau v. Nichols,* 414 U. S. 563 (1974); Education Amendments of 1978, Public Law
   95–561, 92 Stat. 2270 (1978); Office for Civil Rights, *Task Force Findings Specifying
   Remedies Available for Eliminating Past Educational Practices Ruled Unlawful under
   "Lau v. Nichols."* (Washington, D.C.: Department of Health, Education, and Welfare,
   1975).

2. Office for Civil Rights, *Task Force Findings.*

3. Most educators, legislators, and lay persons however continued to view bilingual
   education as a compensatory and remedial program targeted at minority children
   who were linguistically deficient. For a history of what Valencia refers to as "deficit
   thinking" in education see Richard R. Valencia, ed., *The Evolution of Deficit Thinking:
   Educational Thought and Practice* (Washington, D.C.: The Falmer Press, 1997).

4. For an overview of the changes made to bilingual education during the first decade
   of its implementation see Guadalupe San Miguel, Jr., "Conflict and Controversy in
   the Evolution of Bilingual Education in the United States—An Interpretation," *Social
   Science Quarterly* 65:2 (June 1984): 506–10.

5. See, for instance, Malcolm N. Danoff, *Evaluation of the Impact of ESEA Title VII
   Spanish/English Bilingual Education Programs* (Palo Alto, CA: AIR, 1978). For a cri-
   tique of the AIR reports see Jose Cardenas, "Response I," in Noel E. Epstein, *Lan-
   guage, Ethnicity and the Schools* (Washington, D.C.: Institute for Educational
   Leadership, 1977), 71–84; Tracy C. Gray and M. Beatriz Arias, *Challenge to the AIR
   Report* (Arlington, VA: Center for Applied Linguistics, 1978); Joan S. Bissell, *A Review
   of the Impact Study of ESEA Title VII Spanish/English Bilingual Education Programs*
   (Sacramento, CA: Office of the Auditor General, State Legislature, 1979); and Robert
   A. Cervantes, *An Exemplary Consafic Chingatropic Assessment: The AIR Report* (Los
   Angeles, CA: National Dissemination and Assessment Center, 1978).

6. Keith A. Baker and Adriana A. de Kanter, *Effectiveness of Bilingual Education: A Review of the Literature* (Washington, D.C.: OPBE, 1981).

7. The most recent study making this argument is C. Rossell and K. Baker, "The Educational Effectiveness of Bilingual Education," *Research in the Teaching of English* 30:1 (1996): 7–74.

8. See, for instance, Max Rafferty, "Bilingual Education: Hoax of the 1980s," *The American Legion* March 1981: 4, 15–16, 39–40; and William Raspberry, "No Sense—In Any Language," *Washington Post*, 22 October 1980, 23A.

9. For an overview of these arguments see Baker and de Kanter, *Effectiveness*. See also Stephen D. Krashen, *Condemned Without a Trial: Bogus Arguments Against Bilingual Education* (Westport, CT: Heinemann, 1999).

10. Other popular arguments were made including that most immigrants succeeded without bilingual education and that the United States was the only country that promotes bilingual education. For a summary of these arguments see Krashen, *Condemned*; and James Crawford, "Ten Common Fallacies About Bilingual Education," *ERIC Digest*, November 1998 (EDO-FL-98-10).

11. Eduardo Hernandez-Chavez, Jose Llanes, Roberto Alvarez, and Steve Arvizu, *The Federal Policy Toward Language and Education: Pendulum or Progress?* Monograph No. 12 (Sacramento, CA: Cross Cultural Resource Center, California State University, 1981). They argue that this report invites the federal government to abrogate its responsibility for providing equal educational opportunity. Stanley S. Seidner, *Political Expediency or Educational Research: An Analysis of Baker and de Kanter's Review of the Literature of Bilingual Education* (Rosslyn, VA: National Clearinghouse for Bilingual Education, 1981).

12. U.S. General Accounting Office, *Bilingual Education: A New Look at the Research Evidence* (Washington, D.C.: GPO, March 1987); James Crawford, *At War with Diversity: U.S. Language Policy in an Age of Anxiety* (Buffalo, NY: Multilingual Matters, 2000); James Crawford, "Ten Common Fallacies"; Jay Greene, *A Meta-Analysis of the Effectiveness of Bilingual Education* (Claremont, CA: Tomás Rivera Center, 1998).

13. Stephen D. Krashen, *Under Attack: The Case Against Bilingual Education* (Culver City, Ca.: Language Education Associates, 1996); Crawford, "Ten Common Fallacies"; and Krashen, *Condemned*.

14. See Allan C. Ornstein, "The Changing Federal Role in Education," *American Education* 20 (December 1984): 4–7. See also Jack H. Shuster, "Out of the Frying Pan: The

Politics of Education in a New Era," *Phi Delta Kappan* (May 1982): 583–91. A primary objective of his administration was to limit the role of the federal government. In keeping with this philosophy, Reagan and his congressional allies mounted an attack against bilingual education. See Ira Shor, *Culture Wars: School and Society in the Conservative Restoration, 1969–1984* (New York: Routledge and Kegan Paul, 1986).

15. This data can be gleaned from the following reports: *Strengthening Bilingual Education: A Report from the Commissioner of Education to the Congress and the President* (Washington, D.C.: USOE, DHEW, June 1979) and *The Condition of Bilingual Education in the Nation, 1984: A Report from the Secretary of Education to the President and the Congress* (Washington, D.C.: USDOE, 1984).

16. National Advisory and Coordinating Council on Bilingual Education, *Tenth Annual Report* (Washington, D.C.: US Dept of Education, March 1986); James L. Lyons, "The View from Washington," *NABE News X* (Fall 1986): 11, 15.

17. *Address by William J. Bennett, U.S. Secretary of Education to the Association for a Better New York.* New York, New York, September 26, 1985. (In author's possession.)

18. "Notice of Proposed Rulemaking," *Federal Register*, 50, no. 226 (Friday, Nov. 22, 1985): 48352–48370.

19. For a detailed view of these and other actions illustrating "a declining federal leadership in promoting equal educational opportunity" between 1980 and 1982 see "U.S. Commission on Civil Rights Addresses Educational Inequities," *IDRA Newsletter* (April 1982): 1–8. A general interpretation of the changing nature of the federal role in education under the Reagan Administration is provided by Shuster, "Out of the Frying Pan," and by Ornstein, "The Changing Federal Role."

20. James Crawford, "Bilingual Program Grantees Told to Cut Travel, Salary Expenses," *Education Week*, 11 June 1986, 10 and "'Mainstreaming' Is Factor in Bilingual Grant Awards, Official Says," *Education Week*, 22 Oct 1986, 6. A copy of this action is found in "Text of Civil Rights Office Letters to Regional Heads, School Districts," Education Week, 27 Nov, 1985, 16. See also James Hertling, "Flexibility Stressed in New Rules for Bilingual Classes," *Education Week*, 27 Nov 1985, 1, 16.

21. James Crawford, "Bennett's Plan for Bilingual Overhaul Heats Up Debate," *Education Week*, 12 Feb 1986, 1, 22; Lee May, "Latinos Assail Bilingual Education Plans," *Los Angeles Times*, 25 Jan 1986, part I, 3; Office of Research Advocacy and Legislation, *Secretary Bennett's Bilingual Education Initiative: Historical Perspectives and Implications* (Washington, D.C.: National Council of La Raza, Oct 31, 1985); James

L. Lyons, "Education Secretary Bennett on Bilingual Education: Mixed Up or Malicious?" *CABE Newsletter,* 8:2 (October/November 1985): 1, 15.

22. Ironically, while they limited the types of students who could enroll in bilingual education programs, opponents expanded the coverage to include the diverse groups of immigrants coming to this country, especially those from Latin America, the Caribbean, and Asia. (Author's note.)

23. Officially, there were five fundable programs. Three of these were instructional programs for LEP children—Transitional Bilingual Education (TBE), Developmental Bilingual Education (DBE), and Special Alternative Instructional Programs (SAIP). The first two allowed for native language instruction, the latter one did not. See *Bilingual Education Act,* Public Law 98–511 (October 19, 1984).

24. *Bilingual Education Act,* Public Law 100–297 (April 28, 1988).

25. *The No Child Left Behind Act,* Public Law 107–110 (August 3, 2001).

26. See "House OKs School Reform Bill," *Houston Chronicle,* 14 Dec, 2001, 10A.

27. Jeffrey J. Kuenzi, *Education of Limited English Proficient and Recent Immigrant Students: Provisions in the No Child Left Behind Act of 2001* (Washington, D.C.: Congressional Research Service, the Library of Congress, March 1, 2002), 1.

28. For two different responses to the Elementary and Secondary Education Act in general and the bilingual education bill in particular by supporters of this program see National Council of La Raza, "Statement of Raul Yzaguirre on the Elementary and Secondary Education Act," December 14, 2001, pp. 1–2 (in author's possession) and James Crawford, "Obituary: The Bilingual Education Act, 1968–2002." N.d., *http://www.ourworld.compuserve.com/homepages/JWCRAWFORD/new.htm.* The former praises the bipartisan approach to the enactment of this bill and does not critique the new bill but cautions that the changes need to be more effectively monitored by the federal government; the latter argues that the new bill dismantles the federal Title VII program and turns most funding decisions over to the states.

29. Josué M. González, "Editor's Introduction: Bilingual Education and the Federal Role, "If Any . . . ," *Bilingual Research Journal* 26:2 (Summer 2002), ix.

30. Ornstein, "The Changing Federal Role." See also Shuster, "Out of the Frying Pan."

31. For a history of English-only movements in the U.S. see James Crawford, *Hold Your Tongue: Bilingualism and the Politics of "English Only"* (New York: Addison-Wesley Publishing Company, 1992). See also James Crawford, *Language Loyalties: A Source Book on the Official English Controversy* (Chicago: University of Chicago Press, 1992).

32. For Bush's proposals on bilingual education in particular and education in general see Erik W. Robelen, "Bush Plan: No Child Will Be Left Behind—Democrats, GOP Agree in Principle on Federal Role," *Education Week,* 31 January 2001, 1, 24. For a view of these proposed changes see Mary Ann Zehr, "Bush plan could alter bilingual education," *Education Week on the Web,* February 21, 2001, pp. 1–6. *www.edweek. org/ew/ewstory.cfm?slug=23biling.h20.*

33. For a view of NABE's views on this legislation in early August see *NABE Action Alert: Congress Appoints Conferees on Legislation Governing Federal Bilingual Education,* August 2, 2001, pp. 1–7. (in author's possession). For a copy of this bill see *No Child Left Behind, Title III,* August 3, 2001. (pp. 270-315). *www.ed.gov/inits/nclb/part7. html.*

EPILOGUE

What is the state of federal policy for the education of Limited English Proficient (LEP) children two years after the passage of the No Child Left Behind Act? One way to characterize this policy is that it is in flux but several trends have already emerged.

First, there is a pervasive ignorance of the bill's provisions among parents and the general public. Most parents and a variety of groups interested in education, e.g., the League of United Latin American Citizens or LULAC, are not aware of the bill's provisions as they relate to LEP children. Many of them still think that federal policy is supportive of native language instruction. More importantly, however, there is a general acceptance among the majority of teachers, administrators, and school officials of the bill's provisions, especially the English-only mandates. Educators involved in submitting grants, for the most part, do not care much about the merits of bilingual vs. monolingual instruction. They are primarily interested in receiving federal funds to establish a variety of programs aimed at meeting the needs of LEP children. In many cases, these individuals consider themselves professional educators interested in educating LEP children by utilizing whatever the federal government approves, even if it is wrong. A few educators, on the other hand, do care and have the will to challenge the federal government's directives. These individuals use a variety of creative mechanisms to challenge, reinterpret, or subvert the assimilationist and culturally conformist intentions of the new federal law. More research, however, will need to be made to discover these individuals and how they are framing their programs in the current period of conservatism in education.

Second, federal educational policy for LEP children has remained under the control and influence of English-only advocates. The supporters of native language instruction, in other words, have been effectively excluded from the administration and operation of federal educational programs for LEP children. Those in charge of formulating and implementing policy at the federal level avidly oppose the use of native language instruction in the education of LEP children and fiercely support the use of English-only language approaches with these children. Thus there is no clash between the desires of the President, the Secretary of Education, and the Director and staff of the Office of English Language Instruction. Unanimity of thought on the issue of language, in combination with the exclusion of supporters of native language instruction, has guided the implementation of federal policy on the education of LEP children during the past several years.

Third, federal educational policy for LEP children has been converted from a competitive grant program to a formula grant program. The funds and responsibility for awarding grants to local educational agencies and other eligible entities have shifted from the federal to the state level. This means that the majority of funds for the establishment of educational programs for LEP children are now found at the state level rather than at the national level.[1] Under Title III of the No Child Left Behind Act, federal funds for the education of LEP children are distributed to the fifty states, the District of Columbia, and Puerto Rico based on proportions of their LEP and recent immigrant populations relative to national counts of these populations. Because of this new funding formula, state educational agencies rather than federal educational ones have the funds desired by local school officials. They also decide who gets the funds. Therefore, the politics of decision-making is now based on the particular dynamics of state and local developments rather than national ones.

Fourth, the distribution of federal programs for the instruction of LEP kids has been bureaucratized. Those in charge of distributing the funds in the state educational agencies, in other words, are not interested in debating the merits of particular ways of teaching LEP children. Their primary concern, as professional bureaucrats, is to implement federal policy, in this case Title III of the No Child Left Behind Act, in the most efficient way possible.

Despite the emergence of these trends, one thing is certainly clear, federal policy on the education of LEP children does not support the use of native language instruction. The failure to recognize the important role native language instruction plays in the education of LEP children will certainly create obstacles for the success of this policy. The demand for bilingual education, i.e., for native language instruction, however, will continue even if policy fails to acknowledge it.

NOTES

1. The federal government still controls funds for awarding continuation grants and professional development grants. For an overview of these funds, see Jeffrey J. Kuenzi, *Education of Limited English Proficient and Recent Immigrant Students: Provisions in the No Child Left Behind Act of 2001,* (CRS Report for Congress) (Washington, D.C.: Congressional Research Service, 2002).

EXTENDED BIBLIOGRAPHIC ESSAY

INTRODUCTION

The following is an extended bibliographic essay of the primary and secondary sources written from 1960 to 2001 that can be used to do an in-depth history of this policy. The essay is organized into the three major stages of the policy-making cycle as discussed by James E. Anderson: the formation, implementation, and impact or evaluation stage.[1] The first stage involves all those factors that influence the development and enactment of policy. The second one focuses on the process of implementing the policy. The final stage emphasizes the evaluation of this policy and the factors that go into the reauthorization of policy. These three stages comprise one policy-making cycle.

Bilingual education policy has gone through six major policy cycles since it was first enacted. In 2001, it entered its seventh policy cycle. Each of these three stages occurred within each policy cycle and repeated themselves in the following ones. The first policy cycle for the federal bilingual education act occurred between 1965 and 1974. It ended with the reauthorization of the bilingual bill in the latter year. Since 1974, this bill has been reauthorized five additional times: 1978, 1984, 1988, 1994, and 2001.

This extended essay discusses pertinent literature related to each aspect of these policy cycles. It also has an introductory section focusing on the important contextual factors of the early 1960s influencing the initial arguments for the development of federal bilingual education policy.

CONTEXTUAL FACTORS IN THE ORIGINS OF FEDERAL BILINGUAL EDUCATION POLICY, 1960–1965

The origins of the contemporary bilingual education movement began in the early 1960s. Although initiated by language specialists and educators involved in the promotion of foreign languages in the elementary schools, several significant developments in the area of bilingual research, the black civil rights movement, federal legislation, and the Chicano movement influenced this incipient movement.

Research on Bilingualism

Bilingualism research questioned two prominent myths in education: the myth of the negative impact of bilingualism on intelligence and academic achievement and the myth of the melting pot thesis or assimilation. For two important articles showing the positive impact of bilingualism on intelligence see Elizabeth Peal and Wallace Lambert, "The Relation of Bilingualism to Intelligence," *Psychological Monographs, General and Applied* 76 (1962): 1–23 and Joshua Fishman, "Bilingualism, Intelligence, and Language Learning," *Modern Language Journal* 49 (March 1965): 227–37. For several important studies showing the positive impact of bilingualism on school achievement see Eleanor Thonis, *Bilingual Education for Mexican American Children: A Report of an Experiment Conducted in Marysville Joint Unified School District, Marysville, California, Oct. 1966–June, 1967* (Sacramento, CA: California Dept. of Education, 1967); NEA, *Pero No Invencibles—The Invisible Minority* (Washington, D. C.: NEA, Dept. of Rural Supervision, 1966); and Wallace E. Lambert and G. Richard Tucker, *Bilingual Education of Children: The St. Lambert Experiment* (Rowley, MA: Newbury House Publishers, Inc., 1972).

A. Cohen, *A Sociolinguistic Approach to Bilingual Education* (Rowley, MA: Newbury House Publishers, Inc., 1976) aptly summarized the new findings on bilingualism and learning of the 1960s. He noted that by the end of this decade the Spanish-speaking children instructed bilingually, the term used for English-language learners then, tended to perform as well in English language skills and in the content areas as comparable students taught only in English. At the same time, he added, these children were developing language skills in Spanish. Anglo students in bilingual programs, in turn, did not appear adversely affected in their English language development and in the content subjects, and were learning a second language, Spanish.

Research on bilingualism also raised questions about assimilation. Scholars found that certain minority groups, especially the Spanish- and French-speaking, maintained their language abilities and cultural identity over time. They, in other words, were not melting. See, for instance, Joshua Fishman, "The Status and Prospects of Bilingualism in the U.S.," *Modern Language Journal* 49 (March 1965): 143–155; Chester C. Christian, Jr., "The Acculturation of the Bilingual Child," *Modern Language Journal* 69 (March, 1965): 160–65; and Joshua Fishman, *Language Loyalty in the United States* (The Hague: Mouton, 1966). For more general information on the myth of the melting pot in the U.S. see Nathan Glazer and Danial Moynihan, *Beyond the Melting Pot: The Negroes, Puerto Ricans, Jews, Italians, and Irish of New York City* (Cambridge, MA: M.I.T. Press, 1963).

Civil Rights Movement

A second important factor in the support for bilingual education during the mid-1960s was the growing strength of the black civil rights movement. This movement focused attention on the various forms of discrimination in American life and suggested new means for eliminating discriminatory policies and practices, including the use of protest, demonstrations, and pickets. For an overview of this period see Joel Spring, "Civil Rights," in *The Sorting Machine Revisited* (New York: Longman, 1989), 111–16; Diane Ravitch, "Race and Education," in *The Troubled Crusade* (New York: Basic Books, Inc., 1983), 114–44; and especially Harvard Sitkoff, *The Struggle for Black Equality: 1954–1992*, Revised ed. (New York: Hill and Wang, 1993).

In addition to race, Americans realized that discrimination was also based on other factors including ethnicity. In the case of Spanish-speaking children, civil rights leaders and educators began to emphasize the impact and significance of ethnic discrimination on academic success. These individuals argued that discrimination against Spanish-speaking children in general and the suppression of their language in particular, in addition to other factors, caused underachievement. Discrimination also led to the waste of necessary national language resources that could benefit the country. For examples of some of these studies see Joshua Fishman, "Childhood Indoctrination for Minority Group Membership," *Daedalus* 90:2 (Spring 1961): 329–49; Mildred V. Boyer, "Texas Squanders Non-English Resources," *Texas Foreign Language Association Bulletin* 5:3 (Oct 1963): 1–8; and Mildred V. Boyer, "Poverty and the Mother Tongue," *Educational Forum* 29:3 (March 1965): 290–96.

Social Legislation

Increased federal involvement in education in general and the government's poverty legislation in particular also reinforced the need for bilingual education. This legislation renewed consideration of poverty and educational underachievement among Spanish-speaking minority children. Two of the most important statutes enacted during these years were the Economic Opportunity Act of 1964 and the Elementary and Secondary Act of 1965. For a discussion of the importance of the War on Poverty and the role played by the Elementary and Secondary Education Act of 1965 see Spring, "War on Poverty," in *The Sorting Machine Revisited* (New York: Longman, 1989), 186–229.

The War on Poverty legislation encouraged scholars to focus on the factors impacting school performance among poor children of color residing in ghettos, barrios, and reservations. Those interested in the education of ethnic Mexican and Latino children, argued that, in addition to poverty and alienation, discrimination against these children in general and the suppression of Spanish in particular, also caused underachievement. For a summary of the role that poverty and discrimination played in the education of Mexican Americans see Thomas P. Carter, *Mexican Americans in School* (New York: College Entrance Examination Board, 1970). See also Herschel T. Manuel, *Spanish-speaking Children of the Southwest* (Austin: University of Texas Press, 1965).

Activists and Cultural Pluralism

Chicano and Chicana activism also impacted the bilingual education movement. These activists challenged the cultural and political hegemony of the dominant groups and promoted significant educational reforms aimed at improving the academic success of Mexican American children. The effort for improved school success of poor Mexican-American children was concentrated in the struggle for bilingual education in the United States. For an overview of the Chicano Movement's ideals see Ignacio M. Garcia, *Chicanismo: The Forging of a Militant Ethos Among Mexican Americans* (Tucson: University of Arizona Press, 1997). For more general histories of this movement and its relationship to education see the following: Guadalupe San Miguel, Jr., *Brown, Not White: School Integration and the Chicano Movement* (College Station: Texas A & M University Press, 2001); Rubén Donato, *The Other Struggle for Equal Schools: Mexican Americans During the Civil Rights Era* (Albany, NY: State University of New York Press, 1997); Armando Trujillo, *Chicano Empowerment and Bilingual Education: Movimiento Politics in Crystal City, Texas* (New York: Garland Publishing, Inc., 1998); Carlos Munoz, Jr., *Youth, Identity, Power: The Chicano Movement* (New York: Verso, 1989); Armando Navarro, *Mexican American Youth Organization: Avant-Garde of the Chicano Movement in Texas* (Austin: University of Texas Press, 1995); and Armando Navarro, *The Cristál Experiment: A Chicano Struggle for Community Control* (Madison, WI: The University of Wisconsin Press, 1998). For examples of the uses of education for school reform see Manuel Ramirez III, "Bilingual Education as a Vehicle for Institutional Change," in Alfredo Castaneda, et al., eds, *Mexican Americans and Educational Change* (New York: Arno Press, 1974), 387–407; Atilano A. Valencia, "Bilingual-Bicultural Education: A Quest for Institutional Reform," *Spring Bulletin* (Riverside, CA: Western Regional Desegregation Projects, University of California, Riverside, California, April, 1971): 11; Carlos E. Cortés, "Revising the 'All-American Soul Course': A Bicultural Avenue to Educational Reform," in Alfredo Castaneda, et al., eds, *Mexican Americans and Educational Change* (New

York: Arno Press, 1974), 314–39; and Atilano A. Valencia, "Bilingual Education: A Quest for Bilingual Survival," in Alfredo Castaneda, et al., eds, *Mexican Americans and Educational Change* (New York: Arno Press, 1974), 345–62.

THE INITIAL YEARS
Formation
These contextual factors eventually led to specific strategies for enacting bilingual education legislation. To begin the process, educators issued an important report that defined the problem of psychosocial adaptation and academic underachievement among Mexican Americans and laid the foundations for using bilingual instruction as a solution. For a copy of this report see NEA, *Pero No Invencibles—The Invisible Minority* (Washington, D. C.: NEA, Dept. of Rural Supervision, 1966). This report studied the dimensions of the problem confronting schools with large numbers of Spanish-speaking children and developed solutions based on the use of bilingualism.

The NEA report came to the attention of policymakers at a national conference called by the National Education Association in 1966. *Las Voces Nuevas del Sudoeste: A Symposium on The Spanish-speaking Child in the Schools of the Southwest, Tucson, Arizona, October 30–31, 1966* (Tucson, Arizona: National Education Association, Committee on Civil And Human Rights of Educators of the Commission on Professional Rights and Responsibilities, 1966), summarizes the issues raised at the conference. At this conference the survey findings were discussed, new efforts to educate Spanish speaking children were demonstrated, and a blueprint for further action at all levels of government was developed.

As a result of these efforts legislators introduced bilingual education at the federal level in 1967 and later in different states. U.S. Senator Ralph Yarborough (D-Texas) initiated these efforts when he introduced the first bilingual education bill at the federal level in 1967. Ralph Yarborough, "Two proposals for a Better Way of Life for Mexican Americans in the Southwest," *Congressional Record* (January 17, 1967): 599–600, provides some introductory remarks on this bill and on its need.

The following set of congressional reports and hearings provides a wealth of information on the actors involved in bilingual policymaking as well as on the rationale and need for bilingual education among the hundreds of individuals who contributed to its enactment. The congressional reports are U.S. Sen., Committee on Labor and Public Welfare, *Elementary and Secondary Education Act Amendments of 1967, Report No. 90–726* (90th Cong., 1st Sess.) and House of Rep., Committee on Education and Labor, *Elementary and Secondary Education Act Amendments of 1967, Report No. 90–1049* (90th Cong., 1st Sess.) The congressional hearings important in the enactment of bilingual education legislation are: U.S. Sen., *Bilingual Education, Hearings before the Special Subcommittee on Bilingual Education of the Committee on Labor and Public Welfare on S. 428* (2 vols.) (90th Cong., 1st Sess.) and House of Rep., *Bilingual Education Programs, Hearings before the General Subcommittee on Education of the Committee on Education and Labor on H.R. 9840 and H.R. 10224* (90th Cong., 1st Sess.).

The process of adopting the Bilingual Education Act of 1968 has been studied by the following authors: Gilbert Sanchez, "An Analysis of the Bilingual Education Act, 1967–1968" (Ph.D. diss., University of Massachusetts, 1973); Elliot Lewis Judd, "Factors Affecting the Passage of the Bilingual Education Act of 1967" (Ph.D. diss., New York University, 1977); Abdul Karim Bangura and Martin C. Muo, *United States Congress and Bilingual Education* (New York: Peter Lang, 2001); Michael Joseph Croghan, "Title VII of 1968: Origins, Orientations and Analysis" (Ph.D. diss., University of Arizona, 1997); and Martin Chuks Muo, "The Passage of the 1968 Bilingual Education Act and Its Aftermath: A Legislative Systems Analysis" (Ph.D. diss., Howard University, 1994). Select aspects of the adoption process can also be found in Paul Stoller, "The Language Planning Activities of the U.S. Office of Bilingual Education," *International Journal of the Sociology of Language* 11 (1976): 45–60; "Bilingual Education," *New Republic,* 21 Oct 1967: 9–10; "Correspondence," *New Republic* 18 Nov 1967: 44–45; Francesco M. Cordasco, "Knocking Down the Language Walls: Proposed Amendment to ESEA to Establish Bilingual Education Programs," *Commonweal* 6 Oct 1967: 6–8; Francesco M. Cordasco,

"Educational Enlightenment Out of Texas," *Teachers College Record* 71: 4 (May 1970): 639–42, and Ralph W. Yarborough, "Perspectives on the First National Bilingual Education Act," in *Compendium of Readings in Bilingual Education: Issues and Practices* (San Antonio: Texas Association for Bilingual Education, 1994), 1–3.

The final bill, passed in December 1967 and signed into law in January 1968, was the Bilingual Education Act, officially referred to as Public Law 90–247, 81 *Stat.* 816, (1968).

Implementation

1. Funding/legislation

For a year and a half after its enactment, no funding was provided for bilingual education. Joshua Fishman, "The Politics of Bilingual Education," in Francesco M. Cordasco, ed, *Bilingual Schooling in the U.S.* (New York: McGraw-Hill Book Company, 1976), 141–49, provides an explanation of the reason for no funds. Herman Badillo, "The Politics and Realities of Bilingual Education," *Foreign Language Annals* 5:3 (March 1972): 297–301, provides a similar analysis of the need to influence not only the authorization process but the appropriations process as well. Ralph Yarborough, Senator from Texas, in a December 1968 address to the joint conventions of the Modern Language Association and the American Council on the Teaching of Foreign Languages, discusses the lack of funding and the need for amendments to the existing legislation. See Ralph Yarborough, "Bilingualism as a Social Force," in Bernard Spolsky, ed., *The Language Education of Minority Children* (Rowley, MA: Newbury House Publishers, Inc. 1972), 77–82.

2. Regulations

Regulations governing the implementation of bilingual education were developed in 1969, 1971, 1973, and 1974. The first set of regulations was issued in 1969 and appeared as "Financial Assistance for Bilingual Education Programs," *Federal Register* 34, no. 4 (7 Jan. 1969): 201–5. The second set appeared as U.S. Office of Education, *Programs Under*

Bilingual Education Act: Manual for Project Applicants and Grantees (Washington, D.C.: GPO, 1971). The third and fourth sets appeared as "Bilingual Education Act, Regulations," *Federal Register*, 38, no. 189 (1 Oct 1973): 27223–27227 and "Bilingual Education Guidelines," *Federal Register* 39, no. 100 (22 May 1974): 17963, respectively.

3. Issues in implementation

The implementation of bilingual education legislation, once funded, was tension-riddled, chaotic and poorly conducted. Several reports on the status of bilingual education implementation are available. Garland Cannon, "Bilingual Problems and Developments in the United States," *PMLA 86* (May 1971): 452–58, discusses the status of bilingual education during the first two years of its implementation (1969–1971). He argues that there are three lacks in bilingual education implementation: a lack of evaluation, a lack of programs, and a lack of purpose in the shaping of bilingual policies. Theodore Andersson, "Bilingual Education: The American Experience," *Modern Language Journal* 55 (Nov. 1971): 427–40, provides a description of the origins and status of bilingual education programs in the U.S. up to 1972. He concludes that the lack of public support for language maintenance and cultural pluralism, the lack of adequately trained teachers, and unresolved questions relating to pedagogy and the uses of non-English languages to achieve these instructional goals are several formidable obstacles to effective implementation. Maria M. Swanson, "Bilingual Education: The National Perspective," in Gilbert A. Jarvis, ed., *The ACTFL Review of Foreign Language Education* 5 (Skokie, IL: National Textbook, 1974), 75–127, provides a comprehensive albeit disorganized essay of the political, programmatic, and philosophical developments in bilingual education. Emphasis is placed on the years 1972 and 1973. Lawrence Wright, "Bilingual Education Movement at the Crossroads," in Earl J. Ogletree and David Garcia, eds., *Education of the Spanish Speaking Child* (Springfield, IL: Charles C. Thomas, 1975), 335–45 (originally appeared in *Phi Delta Kappan* 60 [Nov 1973]: 187–89), provides an analysis of the status of the bilingual education movement in 1973 and discusses the lack of funds, legislative developments in bilingual education at the federal and state level, and additional areas that could create problems in the future. John C. Molina, "Bilingual Education in U.S.A.," in Rudolph C. Troike and Nancy Modiano, eds., *Proceedings of the First Inter-American Conference on Bilingual Education* (Arlington, VA: CAL, 1975), 25–31, provides a brief status report on bilingual education five years after its passage. He argues that bilingual education faces four major policy issues: to eradicate the concept of "disadvantaged," to introduce the maintenance approach to national policy on bilingual education, to increase curriculum and instructional materials, and to upgrade teacher training.

Policymakers dealt with several policy issues during these early years that were largely defined by bilingual education advocates. First, there were issues pertaining to the goals of bilingual education and whether this program should be aimed at promoting bilingualism or English fluency. Issues around bilingualism and its relationship to education were vigorously debated. A. Bruce Gaarder, "Bilingual Education: Central Questions and Concerns," in Hernan La Fontaine, ed., *Bilingual Education* (Wayne, NJ: Avery Publishing Group, Inc., 1978), 33–38, raises specific issues about the nature of bilingualism and its relationship to education. Robert F. Roeming, "Bilingualism and the National Interest," *Modern Language Journal* 55 (Feb. 1971): 73–81, argues that the issue is not one of language but of economic deprivation.

A second major policy issue was related to three key programmatic concerns in implementing bilingual education: personnel, curriculum development, and to some extent, evaluation. Most scholars touch upon other themes in addition to these three but they all agree that the latter are overlapping ones. See Andersson, "Bilingual Education"; Swanson, "Bilingual Education"; Wright, "Bilingual Education"; and Molina, "Bilingual Education," listed above.

One of the most important documents to discuss these issues was the study conducted by the Comptroller General of the U.S. This report, The Comptroller General of the U.S., *Bilingual Education: An Unmet Need* (Washington, D.C.: GPO, 1976), 1–29, provides an overview of Congress' intention in enacting the bilingual education bill and of the

Office of Education's (OE) major responsibilities in achieving the goals stipulated. It evaluates the Office of Education's efforts in meeting the goals of identifying effective instructional approaches to educating LEP children, training bilingual teachers, and developing suitable instructional materials for these programs set by the bilingual bill. It finds that OE has made little progress in each of these areas and proposes recommendations for improving the Office of Education's efforts in program implementation.

A final policy issue to emerge in the implementation of bilingual education legislation pertained to the federal role in this program. The primary issue was whether the federal government should play a limited or expansive role in bilingual education. A limited role implied decreased federal funding for this program and a dependence on transitional bilingual education aimed at promoting English fluency. An expansive role implied increased federal funding for bilingual education, support of maintenance bilingual education, promotion of cultural pluralism, and increased involvement in funding of "capacity-building" activities such as teacher training, research, and curriculum development. Susan G. Schneider, "The Development of the Administration Position on Bilingual Education," in *Reform, Revolution, or Reaction: The 1974 Bilingual Education Act* (New York: Las Americas, 1976), 99–120, provides an excellent overview of these key policy issues during the period from 1965 to 1974.

4. Compliance

Early on the implementation of bilingual education programs was concerned with compliance of civil rights procedures. The basis for civil rights concerns in bilingual education can be found in the U.S. Department of Health, Education, and Welfare, Office for Civil Rights, "Identification of Discrimination and Denial of Services on the Basis of National Origin," *Federal Register* 35, no. 139 (18 July 1970): 11595–6, a federal regulation interpreting the 1964 Civil Rights Act prohibition on national origin discrimination. Three authors have provided a history of the development of the May 25th Memo and its importance to the education of Mexican Americans. They are James V. Gambone, "Bilingual Bicultural Educational Civil Rights: The May 25th Memo and Oppressive School Practices" (Ph.D. diss., University of New Mexico, 1973); Blandina Cardenas, "Defining Equal Access to Educational Opportunity for Mexican-American Children: A Study of Three Civil Rights Actions Affecting Mexican American Students" (Ed.D. diss., University of Massachusetts, 1974); and Martin H. Gerry, "Cultural Freedom in the Schools: The Right of Mexican American Children to Succeed," in Alfredo Castaneda, et al., eds., *Mexican Americans and Educational Change* (New York: Arno press, 1974), 226–54.

This period of early civil rights issues in bilingual education implementation culminated with the Supreme Court decision of *Lau v. Nichols,* 414 U.S. 563, that upheld the legality of the May 25th memo. The Supreme Court ruled in *Lau* that federally aided school districts had to take affirmative steps in order to address the needs of their non-English-speaking students. This landmark case laid the legal basis for bilingual education and was discussed in a variety of legal and non-legal journals including the following: Christopher Reeber, "Linguistic Minorities and the Right to an Effective Education," *California Western International Law Journal* 3 (1972): 112–32; U.S. Civil Rights Commission, "The Constitutional Right of Non-English Speaking Children to Equal Educational Opportunity," in *A Better-Chance to Learn: Bilingual-Bicultural Education* (Washington, D.C.: GPO, 1975), 142–70; E. Grubb, "Breaking the Language Barrier: The Right to Bilingual Education," *Harvard Civil Rights—Civil Liberties Law Review* 9 (1974): 52–94; W. Johnson, "The Constitutional Right of Bilingual Children to an Equal Educational Opportunity," *Southern California Law Review* 47:3 (May 1974): 943–97; Joseph Montoya, "Bilingual-Bicultural Education: Making Equal Educational Opportunity Available to National Origin Minority Children," *Georgetown University Law Journal* 61 (1973): 991–1007; S. Sugarman and E. Widdess, "Case Commentary: Equal Protection for Non-English-Speaking School Children—Lau v. Nichols," *California Law Review* 62 (1974): 157–82.

Evaluation/Impact

The bilingual education act had a differential impact on state legislation, language use, academic achievement of the LEP children, and community empowerment.

The enactment of the federal bilingual education bill encouraged several states to repeal their English-only laws and to enact their own bilingual bills. Between 1968 and 1974, for example, sixteen states either repealed their English-only laws or else enacted their own bilingual education acts. Heinz Kloss, *Laws and Legal Documents Relating to Problems of Bilingual Education in the U.S.* (Washington, D.C.: ERIC ED 044 703, 1971) and H.M. Geffert, et al., *The Current Status of U.S. Bilingual Education Legislation* (Arlington, VA: Center for Applied Linguistics, 1975) both provide a summary of these bills. Jose Vega, *Politics and Bilingualism in Texas, 1969–1980* (Washington, D.C.: University of America Press, 1983) and Guadalupe San Miguel, Jr., "Bitter Struggles," in National Association for Chicano Studies, *The Chicano Struggle: Past and Present* (New York: Bilingual Review Press, 1983), 111–30, both provide an historical overview of the making of bilingual education legislation in Texas from 1965 to 1980.

Rolf Kjolseth, "Bilingual Education Programs in the United States: Assimilation or Pluralism?" in Bernard Spolsky, ed., *The Language Education of Minority Children* (Rowley, MA: Newbury House Publishers, Inc., 1972), 94–121, critically examines the goals and effects of bilingual education programs in the United States. He argues that the vast majority of them, approximately eighty percent, were aimed at discouraging the use of the child's native language and at facilitating language shift among these children. A. Bruce Gaarder, "The First Seventy-six Bilingual Education Projects," in James E. Alatis, ed., *Bilingualism and Language Contact* (Washington, D.C.: Georgetown University Press, 1970), 163–78, reached a similar conclusion.

While the federal bilingual education act affected state legislation and language use, that is, it promoted language shift, it had no significant impact on the academic achievement of LEP children during its early years. The Comptroller General, for instance, reviewed sixteen projects and found that LEP children made fewer gains than English-speaking children in reading and math. It argued that three possible factors were responsible for these results: the dominant language of LEP children might not have been used enough in instruction, the presence of too many English-speaking children in the program, and the difficulty of assessing English language proficiencies in the target population.

For a discussion of the sixteen projects the Comptroller General reviewed see, the Comptroller General, "Factors Affecting Student Achievement," in *Bilingual Education—An Unmet Need* (Washington, D.C.: GPO, 1976), 45–52. For an explanation of the adverse effects of bilingual education on the academic achievement of LEP children see The Comptroller General, "Program Effect on Participating Students," in *Bilingual Education—An Unmet Need* (Washington, D.C.: GPO, 1976), 30–45.

Two other documents provided evaluation of bilingual education programs: Government Accounting Office, *Summary Project of Type of Instruction Received by Students at 46 Schools Enrolled in 28 Bilingual Education Projects Reviewed by GAO* (Washington, D.C.: GPO, 13 Feb. 1973) and the U.S. Commission on Civil Rights, *The Excluded Student: Educational Practices Affecting Mexicans Americans in the Southwest. Report III: Mexican American Education Study* (Washington, D.C.: GPO, 1972). The former study conducted a six-month evaluation of twenty-eight bilingual education projects. The latter report was part of a comprehensive study of Mexican-American education in the southwest. It describes the exclusionary practices of schools in dealing with the unique linguistic and cultural characteristics of Chicano students.

The problem of assessment was a more general one relating to the problems in conducting evaluations of bilingual education programs. G. R. Tucker and Alison D'Anglesan, "Some Thoughts Concerning Bilingual Education Programs," *Modern Language Journal* 55 (Dec. 1971): 491–93, made one of the earliest pleas for collecting evaluative information on bilingual education programs and especially for conducting evaluations of these programs to see if they were working.

POLICY EXPANSION, 1974–1978
Formation

Only one major study on the reauthorization of the Bilingual Education Act of 1994 has been done. Susan Gilbert Schneider, *Revolution, Reaction, or Reform: The 1974 Bilingual Education Act* (New York: Las Americas Publishing Company, Inc, 1976), explores the development of the 1974 bilingual education act and the different political and philosophical positions taken during the hearings on the bill. It asks whether the 1974 law represented a reaction against the experience of the past, a reform of the federal program, or a revolutionary change in the character of the federal role in bilingual education, and argues that it was a reform.

A wealth of information on the participants, rationales, and issues in bilingual education policymaking can be gleaned from various congressional reports and hearings. The following three congressional reports on bilingual education legislation were issued: U.S. Sen., Committee on Labor and Public Welfare, *Education Amendments of 1974, Report No. 93–763* (93rd Cong., 2nd Sess.); House of Rep., Committee on Education and Labor, *Education Amendments of 1974, Report No. 93–1211* (93rd Cong., 2nd Sess.); and House of Rep., Committee on Education and Labor, *Education Amendments of 1974, Report No. 93–805* (93rd Cong., 2nd Sess.). Two Congressional hearings were held. They were: U.S. Sen., *Education Legislation, 1973, Hearings before the Subcommittee on Education of the Committee on Labor and Public Welfare on S. 1539* (93rd Cong., 1st Sess.), *Part 7* and House of Rep., *Elementary and Secondary Education Amendments of 1973, Hearings before the General Sub-committee on Education of the Committee on Education and Labor on H.R. 16, H.R. 69, H.R. 5163, and H.R. 5823* (93rd Cong., 1st Sess.).

The result of the enactment process was Public Law 93–380, 88 Stat. 503 (1974) commonly referred to as the Bilingual Education Act of 1974.

Implementation

1. Funding/legislation

The implementation of the bilingual education bill occurred from 1974 to 1978. During these years funding for the program increased from $58 million to $135 million and the number of programs increased from 383 to 565. No documents exist on the funding aspect of this bill for this period. Data is usually gathered from a variety of sources such as the Comptroller General's Office, *Bilingual Education: An Unmet Need* (Washington, D.C.: GPO, May 19, 1976); *The Condition of Bilingual Education in the Nation—First Report by the U.S. Commissioner of Education to the Congress and the President* (Fall River, MA: National Assessment and Dissemination Center, Nov., 1976), and Schneider, *Reform, Revolution, or Reaction.*

2. Regulations

Two sets of regulations were issued, one in 1974 and the other in 1976. The former is found in "Bilingual Education," *Federal Register* 39, no. 100 (22 May 1974): 17963–17969. The second set of regulations is found in "Bilingual Education Proposed Regulations," *Federal Register* 41, no. 114 (11 June 1976): 23862–23872.

3. Issues in Implementation

George Blanco, "The Education Perspective," in *Bilingual Education: Current Perspectives, Volume 4* (Arlington, VA: Center for Applied Linguistics, 1977), 21–52, provides an excellent overview of programmatic and policy concerns in the implementation of bilingual education during these years. During this period, some of the key policy issues of the early years continued but with several minor changes. This was especially the case with the federal role (should it be limited or expansive), the goals of bilingual education (transitional vs maintenance), and programmatic concerns. The programmatic concerns focused around several major issues including program planning, design, implementation, and evaluation. Cultural concerns emerged as a new issue for public policymakers and practitioners.

4. Compliance: Civil Rights Issues

The bill's implementation was complicated by civil rights concerns. The basis for civil rights concerns in bilingual education as noted earlier was found in the *Lau* decision of 1974. This decision had a significant impact on Congress, the individual states, the lower courts, and bilingual education policy.

The *Lau* decision provided much needed support for the enactment of the 1974 bilingual education act quoted above. It also encouraged members of Congress to encode the Court's major finding into Title II of the Equal Educational Opportunity Act of 1974 (Public Law 93–380, 88 Stat. 514 [1974], Sec. 204). While the measure was primarily an attempt to impose the strongest congressional limitations to date on the use of transportation or "busing" as a means for overcoming discrimination based on race, color, sex, or national origin, the act provided a list of six acts that the Congress defined as constituting a denial of equal educational opportunity. Among them was one that pertained to language barriers. The *Lau* decision was thus made applicable to all school districts, not just those with a sizeable number of non-English speaking children.

The *Lau* decision also accelerated the trend towards enactment of state bilingual education legislation. Before *Lau,* only four states required some form of bilingual instruction and twelve states encouraged it. After *Lau,* the number requiring bilingual education instruction nearly tripled and those encouraging it increased to fifteen. M. Geffert, et al, *The Current Status of U.S. Bilingual Education Legislation* (Arlington, VA: Center for Applied Linguistics, 1975); Development Associates, Inc., *Final Report on A Study of State Programs in Bilingual Education* (Washington, D.C. Office of Planning, Budget, and Evaluation, Office of Education, Department of Health, Education, and Welfare, 1977); and "State Legislation on Bilingual Education," in *Fourth Annual Report,* 1978–1979 (Washington, D.C.: National Advisory Council on Bilingual Education, 1979), 99–146, provide surveys of the different states that enacted their own bilingual bills after *Lau.*

Lau also spawned several additional lawsuits in which bilingual education was mandated as a solution to past discrimination. Several articles surveyed these legal developments during the mid-1970s. Some reviewed case law on bilingual education while others focused on the implementation and enforcement of civil rights provisions affecting language minority students. They were: Center for Applied Linguistics, *Bilingual Education: Current Perspectives, Vol 3–Law* (Arlington, VA: Center for Applied Linguistics, 1973); W. Foster, "Bilingual Education: An Educational And Legal Survey," *Journal of Law and Education* 5 (1976): 149–71; Peter D. Roos, "Bilingual Education: Hispanic Response to Unequal Education," *Law and Contemporary Problems* 42 (1978): 111–40; Herbert Teitelbaum and Richard J. Hiller, "Bilingual Education: The Legal Mandate," *Harvard Educational Review* 47 (May 1977): 138–70.

Most importantly, *Lau* affected bilingual education by shifting the emphasis away from those school districts who had voluntarily submitted proposals for federal funding to those who were out of compliance with the *Lau* decision. Emphasis shifted from programmatic implementation concerns to enforcement and compliance proceedings, from the activities of the Office of Bilingual Education to that of the Office of Civil Rights, from Mexican Americans in particular to language minority students in general.

In order to provide assistance for complying with Lau the federal government took several actions. It initiated a compliance review process for determining whether local school districts were in compliance with the Lau decision. It then published U.S. Department of Health, Education, and Welfare, Office for Civil Rights, *Task Force Findings Specifying Remedies for Eliminating Past Educational Practices Ruled Unlawful Under Lau v. Nichols* (Washington, D.C.: Office for Civil Rights, 1976). This document, commonly referred to as the *Lau* Remedies, outlined suggested remedies that would be considered in compliance with the *Lau* decision, including identification of the students' home or primary language, diagnosis of educational needs and prescription of program selection, curriculum and personnel requirements, prohibition of racial/ethnic isolation, parental notification, and evaluation. Hundreds of local school districts throughout the country were then investigated and asked to submit plans based on the *Lau* Remedies in order for them to be in compliance with the Supreme Court decision. School districts failing to develop plans based on the Lau Remedies were threatened with the withdrawal of all their federal funds. For an example of one school district

forced to develop bilingual education as a result of OCR investigation see
Mary Carol Combs, "Research and Policy: Factors Influencing the Development of Bilingual Education in the Valle Encantado School District
(Arizona)," (Ph.D. diss., The University of Arizona, 1995). In this disser-
tation, the author argues that research findings had little to do with the
establishment of bilingual education in the Valle Encantado School District. Its development was due to an OCR investigation.

Many school districts were unable to implement the *Lau* Remedies
due to their confusing and unclear provisions. Scholars and policymakers
quickly moved to clarify, through research and through the identification
of research needs, some of the issues raised by the implementation of the
Lau Remedies in the schools. The result was a conference on research
and policy implications of the *Lau* decision and its implementation.

Participants at this conference addressed several aspects of the *Lau*
Remedies, especially the following four: assessment of students' primary
language for determining whether bilingual programs were needed,
diagnosis of student learning behaviors and prescription of culturally
and linguistically responsive instructional procedures, program designs
(specification of bilingual program models appropriate to the language
needs and educational level of students), and teacher training (development of personnel staffing and training procedures appropriate to the
prescribed programs).

A few scholars made several key presentations at this conference.
John B. Lum, "U.S. Office of Civil Rights (DHEW) Lau Remedies:
Administrative Feedback," (pp. 215–32) and Maria Torres, "The Five-
Way Input Requisite for Educational Programs-Bilingual and Others,"
(pp. 233–40) both identify some of the administrative problems associated with implementing the *Lau Remedies.* Unclear concepts such as
"learning style," lack of resources and time, lack of acceptable educational programs, the outright exclusion of ESL as a possible alternative,
the inclusion of fluent English-speaking minority students as targeted
for special services, and staffing limitations were concerns raised by
administrators. Edward A. De Avila and Sharon E. Duncan, "A Few
Thoughts About Language Assessment: The Lau Decision Reconsidered,"

(pp. 244–68) discuss questions about language assessment raised by the *Lau* Remedies and suggest that the problem identified by the *Lau* decision may be a much broader one which can only be solved through the simultaneous consideration of linguistic, developmental, and sociocultural factors. Robert A. Cervantes, "Teacher Behaviors and Cultural Responsiveness: Theoretical and Practical Considerations," (pp. 178–98) focuses on the increasing recognition prompted by the *Lau* decision to deal with the cultural aspects of instruction. Finally, Courtney B. Cazden, "Culturally Responsive Education: A Response to Lau Guidelines II," (pp. 10–55), discusses ways of implementing teaching adapted to the children's learning styles. For further information on the emergent themes pertaining to civil rights compliance in bilingual education after 1974 see *Proceedings of National Conference on Research and Policy Implications Lau Task Force Report, June 17–18, 1976* (Austin, TX: Southwest Educational Development Laboratory, 1976).

Some school districts, however, were unwilling to comply with the *Lau* Remedies due to their prescriptive provisions and raised questions about their legality. Were they guidelines, an agency interpretation, or regulations? Answers to these questions would commit the local school agency to specific types of responses. On April 8, 1976, OCR Elementary and Secondary Division director Lloyd Henderson acknowledged that there had been some "misunderstandings concerning the guidelines" and asked regional directors to clear the matter up with their staffs. The *Lau* Remedies, he reminded them, were not a legal mandate but rather a set of guidelines for assistance and school officials were not mandated to follow it. This statement was quoted in *Education Daily,* 9:77 (20 April 1976): 23Q. See also "Bilingual ed not required," *Austin American-Statesman,* 19 April 1976, A9.

Still, several enforcement officials such as Alberto Ochoa, Director Lau General Assistance Center at the Institute for Cultural Pluralism, San Diego State University, insisted that while bilingual education was not mandated, in certain cases, it was the suggested remedy, and "the only educationally sound way of insuring effective participation in the instructional program." The implication of this statement suggested the appropriateness of the *Lau* Remedies in seeking compliance with the *Lau* decision. See *Press Release*, Alberto Ochoa, Director Lau General Assistance Center, Institute for Cultural Pluralism, San Diego State University, April 22, 1976.

Unsatisfied with these types of local responses, some school districts challenged the *Lau* Remedies' legality in court. Alaska was successful in its challenge. In 1978, as part of a settlement in *Northwest Arctic v. Califano, A-77–216* (D. *Alaska*, 1978), Consent Decree, the OCR agreed to publish official regulations that would finally spell out the obligations of school districts to LEP students. For more than two years, OCR worked on the new rules and, after much internal discussion a "Notice of Proposed Rule Making" appeared in *Federal Register* 45, no.152 (5 August 1980): 52052–52076.

Evaluation/Impact

During 1977 and 1978, several evaluative reports casting doubts on the effectiveness of bilingual education appeared. Noel Epstein, *Language, Ethnicity and the Schools: Policy Alternatives for Bilingual-Bicultural Education* (Washington, D.C.: Institute for Educational Leadership, 1977) raised questions about the "bicultural" aspects of bilingual education and whether the federal government should be involved in supporting language maintenance. Malcolm N. Danoff, *Evaluation of the Impact of ESEA Title VII Spanish/English Bilingual Education Programs* (Palo Alto, CA: American Institutes for Research, 1978) added to this growing criticism by providing evidence indicating that bilingual education was not effective. The latter came to be known as the AIR report, a name derived from the initials of the research group responsible for conducting and publishing this report.

The proponents of bilingual education quickly wrote critical responses to these reports. While Jose A. Cardenas, "Response I," in Epstein, *Language, Ethnicity and the Schools,* 71–84, refuted the arguments made by this reporter regarding bilingual education, most of the comments focused on the AIR report. Three representative responses were: Tracy C. Gray and M. Beatriz Arias, *Challenge to the AIR Report*

(Arlington, VA: Center for Applied Linguistics, 1978); Robert A. Cervantes, *An Exemplary Consafic Chingatropic Assessment: The AIR Report* (Los Angeles: National Dissemination and Assessment Center, 1978); and Joan S. Bissell, *A Review of the Impact Study of ESEA Title VII Spanish/English Bilingual Education Programs* (Sacramento, CA: Office of the Auditor General, State Legislature, March 1979).

The strengthening of federal bilingual education continued to impact local and state developments. Of particular importance was the establishment of new or stronger bilingual education policies in different states. One of these was Arizona. For a study describing the impact of federal bilingual education on Arizona see Martin W. Johnson, "The Controversial Issues of Bilingual Education Surrounding the 1968 Bilingual Education Act and Its Effects on the Mexican Americans in the State of Arizona," (Ph.D. diss., Ohio University, 1983). See also Donal M. Sacken and Medina Marcello, Jr., "Investigating the Context of State-Level Policy Formation: A Case Study of Arizona's Bilingual Education Legislation," *Educational Evaluation and Policy Analysis* 12:4 (Winter 1990): 389–402. This latter study provides an interpretation of the events leading to the passage in 1984 of Arizona's new bilingual education legislation.

POLICY CONTAINMENT, 1978–1984
Formation
The AIR Report, in combination with the Epstein study and other forms of negative media coverage, served as general background information on the nature of the problem confronting policymakers. These studies served as points of departure for discussing evolving issues in bilingual education and for proposing remedies to them.

Iris Polk Berke, "Evaluation into Policy: Bilingual Education, 1978" (Ph.d. diss., Stanford University, 1980), and Iris Polk Berke, "Evaluation and Incrementalism: The AIR Report and ESEA Title VII," *Educational Evaluation and Policy Analysis* 52, 1983: 249–256, provide an analysis of the impact of AIR, Epstein, and other forms of negative evaluations on the reauthorization of the Bilingual Education Act of 1978. She also describes the adoption process and the forces contributing to the reauthorization of this controversial bill. Lilliam Margarita Malave-Lopez, "A Case Study of the Bilingual Education Act of 1978: An Example of the Legislative Process in the U.S. Congress" (Ph.D. diss., State University of New York at Buffalo, 1983), and Armando Alfonso Ayala, "A Comparative Analysis of the 1974 Bilingual Education Act with the Recommended Changes by Field Practitioners and the Final 1978 Bilingual Education Act" (Ed.D. diss., University of San Francisco, 1983), likewise provide an analysis of the enactment of the bilingual education bill in 1978. The final bill, *Education Amendments of 1978, Public Law 95–561* (95th Congress, 2nd Session), was passed by both houses in August 1978.

A wealth of information on the actors and issues in bilingual policy-making can be found in the congressional reports and hearings issued during 1978. Three sets of congressional reports were issued: U.S. Sen., Committee on Human Resources, *Educational Amendments of 1978, Report No. 95–856* (95th Cong., 2nd Sess.); House of Rep., Committee on *Education and Labor, Education Amendments of 1978, Report No. 95–1137* (95th Cong., 2nd Sess.); and House of Rep. Committee on Education and Labor, *Education Amendments of 1978, Report No. 95–1753* (95th Cong., 2nd Sess.) (Conference Report). Information on bilingual education issues can be found in the following Congressional Hearings: U.S. Sen., *Education Amendments of 1978, Hearings before the Subcommittee on Education of the Committee on Human Resources on S. 1753* (95th Cong., 1st Sess.) and House of Rep., *Bilingual Education, Hearings before the Subcommittee on Elementary, Secondary, and Vocational Education of the Committee on Education and Labor on H.R. 15* (95th Cong., 1st Sess.).

In a more general vein Noel Epstein, "Bilingual and Bicultural Education: The Role of the Scholar," in James E. Alatis, ed., *Georgetown University Round Table on Languages and Linguistics, 1978* (Washington, D.C.: Georgetown University Press, 1978), 670–74, discusses the scholar's responsibility in policymaking. According to him, there is a tendency of some scholars who are eager to influence public policy to blur the distinction between their scholarship and their ideologies, between what they know and what they believe. He argues that research, as well as journalism, is the search for the truth, regardless of what the findings are or what the impact of these findings might have on political programs.

The result of all this activity was the Bilingual Education Act of 1974. It is officially cited as Public Law 95–561, 92 Stat. 2268 (1978).

Implementation

1. Funding/legislation

Unlike prior years, the funding for bilingual education from 1978 to 1984 decreased from $135 million to $81.6 million. This data can be gleaned from a variety of annual reports issued by the National Advisory Committee on Bilingual Education and by the U.S. Commissioner of Education listed below. The number of basic programs increased from 565 to 589 but there was a decrease in the number of individuals being served. In 1978 slightly over 300,000 LEP students were being served; the number decreased to 182,000 in 1984.

2. Regulations

Several sets of regulations were developed. They are: "Bilingual Education Program: Decision to Develop Regulations," *Federal Register* 44, no. 14 (19 Jan. 1979): 3996–3997; "Bilingual Education: Interim Final Regulations", *Federal Register* 44, no. 62 (29 March 1979): 18906–18917; "Bilingual Education Regulations," *Federal Register* 44, no. 127 (29 June 1979): 38416–38432; "Bilingual Education Program," *Federal Register* 45, no. 67(4 April 1980): 23208–23244; and "Bilingual Education," *Federal Register* 45, no. 152 (5 August 1980): 52052–52076. All of these provide specific ways in which local school districts were supposed to implement the provisions of the bilingual education act.

3. Issues in implementation

Specific information on the administrative and operational policies and practices involved in implementing the bilingual bill can be found in *Strengthening Bilingual Education: A Report from the Commissioner of*

Education to the Congress and the President (Washington, D.C.: USOE, DHEW, June 1979) and in *The Condition of Bilingual Education in the Nation, 1984: A Report from the Secretary of Education to the President and the Congress* (Washington, D.C.: USDOE, 1984). Additional information can be found in the *National Advisory Council on Bilingual Education's annual reports* from 1979 to 1985 (Third to Ninth NACBE Annual Reports). For information on how bilingual education was being implemented in several states during the late 1970s and early 1980s see Alicia Margarita Caban-Wheeler, "Equal Educational Opportunity: A Policy Analysis of Massachusetts Laws Chapter 71A, Transitional Bilingual Education Act and Chapter 766, Education of the Handicapped Act" (Ed.D diss., Harvard University, 1982); Burton Phillip Yin, "A Descriptive Study of Title VII Program Directors in California: Profiles, Problems and Issues" (Ed.D. diss., University of San Francisco, 1982); Barbara Louise Sultemeier, "Assessing the Relationship Between Hispanic Power Structure and Funding of Bilingual Education" (Ph.D. diss., Texas A & M University, 1982). These studies generally found that states were inadequately implementing federal bilingual education mandates or else, as in the case of a few Texas districts, not implementing them at all.

In late 1983, the Secretary of Education added several members to the National Advisory Committee on Bilingual Education who were opposed to bilingual education and who favored English-only approaches, especially immersion methods. Their views on bilingual education can be found in the 1983 and 1984 NACBE annual report, see especially the index of both reports.

4. Compliance

Issues of compliance with civil rights provisions, especially the enforcement of the *Lau* Remedies, continued to complicate the implementation of bilingual education. The federal government, in response to a court decision (*Northwest Arctic v. Califano,* A-77–216 [D. Alaska, 1978]), pressure from special interest groups, and the need for Latino votes in the upcoming presidential elections, published a proposed *Lau* Remedies for public comment in *Federal Register* 45, no. 152 (5 August 1980): 52052–52076. These proposed remedies emphasized the variety of educational approaches available to meet the needs of LEP children.

The response to the proposed *Lau* Remedies was immediate and critical. Max Rafferty, "Bilingual Education: Hoax of the 1980s," The *American Legion*, March 1981, 4, 15–16, 39–40; and William Raspberry, "No Sense—In Any Language," *Washington Post*, 22 October 1980, A23, argued that the Department of Education, by issuing the proposed regulations, was "dictating" the curriculum to local school officials. In "Drop the Bilingual Rules," *Washington Post*, 28 October 1980, A16, the editor of the *Post* argued that the federal government should ensure that the goal of providing equal opportunity was reached, not prescribe the route that had to be taken.

More generally speaking, Tomas M. Saucedo, Lori S. Orum, and Rafael J. Magallan, *Issue Analysis on Bilingual Education and the Lau Regulations* (Washington, D.C.: National Council of La Raza, January 1981) and Tomas Saucedo, Lori Orum, and Rafael Magallan, "Historical and Legislative Perspectives on Bilingual Education and the Lau Regulations," *Agenda* (1981): 10–14, provide a history of the *Lau* regulations, the arguments and responses made to it, and the congressional efforts to undermine the executive branch's authority to enforce constitutional and statutory guarantees.

As a result of this controversy, the proposed Lau Remedies were withdrawn in February 1981. For a sampling of the reasons for their withdrawal and the controversy this caused see "U.S. to Withdraw Bilingual Rules," *Corpus Christi Times*, 2 February 1981, B15; "Bell Acts to Withdraw proposed Bilingual Education Guidelines," *Houston Chronicle*, 3 February 1981, 16B; and "Local Hispanics Rap Reagan's Bilingual Stand," *Corpus Christi Caller*, 3 March 1981, 38.

In April 1982, the Secretary of Education withdrew the existing Lau Remedies. According to David G. Savage, "Bilingual Education Rules Lifted," *Los Angeles Times*, 25 April 1982, 1, 16–17, conservatives quietly applauded while advocates only provided muted protests to this policy shift.

In addition to withdrawing the proposed and actual *Lau* Remedies, the Reagan administration also sought to downgrade the Office for Civil Rights. For a detailed view of these and other actions illustrating "a declining federal leadership in promoting equal educational opportunity" between 1980 and 1982 see "U.S. Commission on Civil Rights Addresses Educational Inequities," *IDRA Newsletter* (April 1982): 1–8. A general interpretation of the changing nature of the federal role in education under the Reagan Administration is provided by Jack H. Shuster, "Out of the Frying Pan: The Politics of Education in a New Era," *Phi Delta Kappan* (May 1982): 583–91; and by Allan C. Ornstein, "The Changing Federal Role in Education," *American Education* 20 (Dec 1984): 4–7. Ornstein argues that there are three basic trends in federal policy in education: a shift in priorities from social to military and business concerns, reduction in federal funds for education, and a growing demise of the goal of egalitarianism as a national policy.

Evaluation/Impact

Inspector General, *Review of Federal Bilingual Education Programs in Texas* (Washington, D.C.: GPO, 1982) provided a critical view of these programs and argued that they were not successful nor were they being implemented as stipulated by law. It asked that Texas refund several million dollars owed the federal government. Response by Congressional leaders was rapid and critical of this report. U.S. Congress, House, Education and Labor, *Committee on Oversight on Texas Bilingual Education Audits* (Washington, D.C.: GPO, July 29, 1982) provided an opportunity for them to criticize the Inspector General and to request a retraction from him for harshly criticizing and demanding repayment from Texas school officials.

Probably the most important evaluation study of bilingual education was the one conducted by two bureaucrats from the Office of Planning, Budget and Evaluation. Keith A. Baker and Adriana A. de Kanter, *Effectiveness of Bilingual Education: A Review of the Literature* (Washington, D.C.: OPBE, 1981) conducted a review of the literature on the effectiveness of bilingual education. They found that bilingual education was not effective and that other approaches, especially immersion programs, were as effective. Other reports such as the *San Diego Grand Jury Report* (San Diego, California, 1984), also indicated that bilingual education was not effective in teaching these children English.

Proponents of bilingual education had three different types of responses to the Baker/de Kanter report. First, they criticized the report's methodological flaws and its conclusions. Eduardo Hernandez-Chavez, Jose Llanes, Roberto Alvarez, and Steve Arvizu, *The Federal Policy Toward Language and Education: Pendulum or Progress?* Monograph No. 12 (Sacramento, CA: Cross Cultural Resource Center, California State University, 1981), for example, provide a critical overview of the programs evaluated by Baker/de Kanter and argue that this report invites the federal government to abrogate its responsiblity for providing equal educational opportunity. Stanley S. Seidner, *Political Expediency or Educational Research: An Analysis of Baker and de Kanter's Review of the Literature of Bilingual Education* (Rosslyn, VA: National Clearinghouse for Bilingual Education, 1981) provides another critical assessment of this report.

A second response to the Baker/de Kanter report was for educators to begin exploring, in more systematic fashion, the structured immersion method and ESL methods and their applicability to the education of LEP children in the United States. *Studies in Immersion* (Sacramento, CA.: California State Department of Education, 1984) provided an easily accessible resource on the theory and practice of immersion programs in Canada and in the United States. It also explored their potential applicability to the education of LEP children in the United States. While some individual scholars such as Fred Genovese, "The Suitability of Immersion Programs for All Children," *Canadian Modern Language Review* 32 (1976): 494–515, supported this method, others such as Eduardo Hernandez-Chavez, "The Inadequacy of English Immersion Education as an Educational Approach for Language Minority Students in the United States," in *Studies in Immersion*, Ibid., 144–83, presented compelling reasons for rejecting it as a possible alternative to bilingual education for LEP children. Anna Uhl Chamot, *The English as a Second Language Literature (ESLIT) Study* (Arlington, VA.: InterAmerica Research Associates,

Inc., 1985) provides a review and synthesis of current literature on ESL as it pertains to public school education in the United States and addressed several policy issues related to the English language development of LEP students in grades K–12. More specifically, it investigated four areas affecting teaching and learning of ESL: instructional approaches, organizational patterns, instructional materials, and language learning theories supporting instructional approaches.

Other issues besides evaluation of its effectiveness were raised during this period. Tom Bethel, "Why Johnny Can't Speak English," *Harper's Magazine* (Feb. 1979): 30–33; John R. Edwards, "Critics and Criticism of Bilingual Education," *Modern Language Journal* 64:4 (Winter, 1980): 409–415; Ricardo Otheguy, "Thinking About Bilingual Education: A Critical Appraisal," *Harvard Educational Review* 52 (1982): 301–14; and Charles R. Foster, "Defusing the Issues in Bilingualism and Bilingual Education," *Phi Delta Kappan* 63:5 (Jan 1983): 342–44, for instance, provide concrete analysis of arguments and counter-arguments in bilingual education. Otheguy, in particular, examines the assumptions of those who argue against the need for bilingual education programs and provides evidence that the appeal of these arguments rests on a reductionist oversimplification of the facts.

Joshua A. Fishman, "Language Policy: Past, Present, and Future," in Shirley B. Heath and Charles A. Ferguson, eds., *Language in the USA* (Cambridge: Cambridge University Press, 1981), 516–26, and Carlos J. Ovando, "Bilingual/Bicultural Education: its Legacy and Its Future," *Phi Delta Kappan* (April 1983): 564–68, both provide general interpretations of the status and future of bilingual education in the United States. Fishman, in particular, argues that while there are three possible options for language choices in the United States—language shift, maintenance, or enrichment—most activities are concentrated in that policy characterized as language shift. Shirley Brice Heath, "Bilingual Education and National Language Policy," in James E. Alatis, ed., *Georgetown University Round Table on Languages and Linguistics* (Washington, D.C.: Georgetown University Press, 1978), 53–66, discusses the history of a national language policy in the United States and the possibilities for and consequences of a national language policy supporting bilingualism. Thomas J. Burns, "Bilingual Education's Future," *Bilingual Journal* 4:4 (Fall 1980): 11–14 discusses ways of increasing the availability, quality, and scope of bilingual education instruction in this country.

A personal critique of bilingual education and affirmative action is made by Richard Rodriguez, *Hunger of Memory* (Boston, MA: D. R. Godine, 1982).

POLICY REDIRECTIONS, 1984–1988
Formation
Several documents influencing the formulation of a reauthorized bilingual education act appeared in the early 1980s. The most controversial was the Baker and de Kanter report mentioned earlier. This report was part of a larger effort to "provide evidence on which to base a reexamination of federal policies," i.e., to discredit various aspects of bilingual education (See Beatrice F. Berman and Alan L. Ginsburg, *Addressing the Needs of Language Minority Children: Issues for Federal Policy* Washington, D.C.: Office of Planning, Budget, and Evaluation, 1981, p. 2). Five other reports examining critical policy areas pertaining to bilingual education were issued by the Office of Planning, Budget, and Evaluation (OPBE). They were: Robert E. Barnes, *Size of the Eligible Language Minority Population* (Washington, D.C.: OPBE, 1981); Alvin S. Rosenthal, Ann M. Milne, Alan L. Ginsburg, Keith A. Baker, *A Comparison of the Effects of Language Background and Socio-Economic Status on Achievement Among Elementary School Students* (Washington, D.C.: OPBE, 1981); Ann M. Milne and Jan M. Gombert, *Students with Primary Language Other Than English: Distribution and Service Rates* (Washington, D.C.: OPBE, 1981); Elizabeth R. Reisner, *The Availability of Bilingual Education Teachers: Implications for Title VI Enforcement and Good Educational Practice* (Washington, D.C.: OPBE, 1981); and Polly Carpenter-Huffman and Marta Samulon, *Case Studies of Delivery and Cost of Bilingual Education* (Washington, D.C.: OPBE, 1981). All of the above papers were originally published in 198l by the OPBE. In 1983, Keith A. Baker and Adriana A. de Kanter, ed., *Bilingual Education: A Reappraisal of Federal Policy* (Lexington,

MA: Lexington Books, 1983) published some of the above papers as well as several others for the general public.

On the basis of these studies, several members of Congress drafted two bilingual education bills. These bills—S. 2002 and S. 2412—redefined bilingual education to allow funding of a greater variety of approaches, especially immersion as suggested by Baker/de Kanter, and sought to target resources to those most in need. These bills as well as the responses to them by their supporters and opposition forces can be found in Congress, Senate, Committee on Labor and Human Resources, *Bilingual Education Amendments of 1981, Hearings Before the Subcommittee on Education, Arts and Humanities of the Committee on Labor and Human Resources on S. 2002,* Ninety-seventh Congress, Second Session on S. 2002 (Washington, D.C.: GPO, April 23, 26, 1982).

In 1983 and 1984, additional bills were formulated and introduced into Congress. Some of these were based on OPBE studies, others were not. In October 1984 a new reauthorized bilingual education bill was signed by President Reagan. While the process involved in adopting the reauthorized bilingual education bill has not been seriously studied, James L. Lyons, "Bilingual Education: The Past and the New Year—A Report from Washington," *CABE Newsletter* 7 (March/April 1985): 1–2, 6, provides an initial analysis of the forces affecting the adoption process in 1984. For a brief look at the last stages of the bilingual education bill adoption process see also "Bilingual Education Update," *NCBE Forum* (June/July, 1984): 6–7.

U.S. Congress, *Education Amendments of 1984, Report 98–1128,* House of Representatives, 98th Congress, 2nd Session. (Washington, D.C.: GPO, Oct 2, 1984): 5–24 provides a congressional rationale and justification of the new bill. The final bill, Education Amendments of 1984, was signed on October 19, 1984, by President Reagan and is an omnibus bill. The Bilingual Education Act of 1984 is Title II of Public Law 98–511, 98 Stat. 2370 (1984). For one interpretation of this bill see Ramon L. Santiago, "Bilingual Education in 1984: A Giant Step Forward," *Caminos* (Nov. 1984): 30–31.

Implementation

1. Funding/legislation

Funding during the years from 1984 to 1986 remained fairly constant at $132 million. In the 1986–1987 fiscal year the funding level for the bilingual education act increased to $143 million. Data on the U.S. Department of Education budget for bilingual education can be found in National Advisory and Coordinating Council on Bilingual Education, *Tenth Annual Report* (Washington, D.C.: US Dept of Education, March 1986). For data on the budget for fiscal year 1987 see "OBEMLA's Budget for Fiscal Year 1987," *NCBE Forum* (March, 1987), 5–6. James L. Lyons, "The View from Washington," *NABE News* 10 (Fall 1986): 11, 15, provides a capsule review of federal legislation and national policy issues affecting the education of language minority Americans. Included in this review is the budget for bilingual education for the 1987 fiscal year.

2. Regulations

Regulations for implementing bilingual education programs were developed in 1985 and reflected the conservative ideology of the new commissioner of education. "Notice of Proposed Rulemaking," *Federal Register* 50, no. 226 (22 Nov. 1985): 48352–48370, provides specific guidelines for implementing the provisions of the 1984 bilingual education bill and stipulates that school districts, among other things, could decrease the amount of native language instruction provided in their federally funded programs. For responses by the proponents of bilingual education to these guidelines see James Crawford, "Bennett's Plan for Bilingual Overhaul Heats Up Debate," *Education Week*, 12 Feb. 1986, 1, 22; Lee May, "Latinos Assail Bilingual Education Plans," *Los Angeles Times*, 25 Jan 1986, part 1, 3; and James Crawford, "Supporting Comments Reveal Animosity Toward Ethnic Groups," *Education Week*, 12 Feb. 1986, 23. Several months later a final set of regulations was issued by the federal government. No major changes had been made. For a copy of these regulations see "Bilingual Education Regulations," *Federal Register* 51, no. 118 (19 June 1986): 22422–22447. See also "Extend Comments,"

Federal Register 51, no. 8 (13 January 1986): 1393, and "Bilingual Education Regulations," *Federal Register* 51, no. 180 (17 Sept 1986): 33000–33002.

3. **Issues in implementation**

Implementation efforts, as mentioned above, were shaped by the appointment of a new Secretary of Education, William Bennett, who sought significant changes in this policy. *Address by William J. Bennett, U.S. Secretary of Education to the Association for a Better New York* (New York, New York, September 26, 1985. In author's possession.), provided the rationale for changes in the implementation strategy. He argued that the purpose of bilingual education had gone astray and the means had become intrusive and overburdening. In an effort to redirect this program to teach English, he proposed new legislative, regulatory, and compliance changes.

The response by those supportive of a strong bilingual education program was rapid and critical. Two examples of responses to Bennett were Office of Research Advocacy and Legislation, *Secretary Bennett's Bilingual Education Initiative: Historical Perspectives and Implications* (Washington, D.C.: National Council of La Raza, Oct 31, 1985) and James L. Lyons, "Education Secretary Bennett on Bilingual Education: Mixed Up or Malicious?" *CABE Newsletter* 8:2 (October/November 1985): 1, 15.

Bennett's ideas on bilingual education were soon incorporated into and reflected in his proposed regulations (see regulations), legislative proposals (see formation below), and administrative actions. The new directions in bilingual policy can be found in *Ninth Annual Report, 1984–1985* (Washington, D.C.: US Dept of Education, 1985) and in *Tenth Annual Report, 1985–1986* (Washington, D.C.: US Dept of Education, 1986). For an overview of other types of administrative and regulatory actions taken by Bennett during this period, see James Crawford, "Bilingual Program Grantees Told to Cut Travel, Salary Expenses," *Education Week*, 11 June 1986, 10, and "'Mainstreaming' Is Factor in Bilingual Grant Awards, Official Says," *Education Week*, 22 Oct 1986, 6.

4. Compliance

Another aspect of Bennett's initiative was in the area of *Lau* enforcement mechanisms or more generally, civil rights compliance. Although having drastically reduced civil rights enforcement mechanisms, efforts were made to undo existing *Lau* agreements. In November 1985, Bennett invited more than 400 school districts to renegotiate longstanding agreements governing their curricula for LEP students. A copy of this action is found in "Text of Civil Rights Office Letters to Regional Heads, School Districts," *Education Week,* 27 Nov. 1985, 16. For additional information on this action as well as that pertaining to the regulations see James Hertling, "Flexibility Stressed in New Rules for Bilingual Classes," *Education Week,* 27 Nov. 1985, 1, 16, and James Crawford, "U.S. Enforcement of Bilingual Plans Declines Sharply," *Education Week,* 4 June 1986, 1.

Implementation was also shaped by several groups opposed to this program. James Crawford, "Conservative Groups Take Aim at Federal Bilingual Programs," *Education Week,* 19 March 1986, 1, describes three specific organizations opposed to bilingual education: Save Our Schools (SOS), the Council for Inter-American Security, and U.S. English. The first group calls for the "repeal" of this federal program, the second links bilingual education to Hispanic "separatism," "cultural apartheid," and the potential for "terrorism in the U.S.," while the third simply calls for the support of English as the official language of this country.

Evaluation/Impact

The proponents of bilingual education responded in various ways to the federal government's new initiatives. In 1985 they issued several reports critical of the federal government's attack on bilingual education. They were: Ann Willig, "A Meta-Analysis of Selected Studies on the Effectiveness of Bilingual Education," *Review of Educational Research* 55:3 (Fall 1985): 269–317; *The Educational Progress of Language Minority Students: Findings from the 1983–1984 NAEP Reading Study* (Washington, D.C.: National Assessment of Educational Progress, December 1985), summarized in James Crawford, "Finn Blasts NAEP's 'Misleading' Report on

Bilingual Services," *Education Week,* 2 April 1986, 1, 14; and *The Longitu-dinal Study of Immersion and Dual Language Instruction Programs for Language Minority Children* (Washington, D.C.: S.R.A. Technologies, 1985).

Congressional and government supporters of bilingual education issued their own reports in 1986 and 1987. In the summer of 1986, Congressman Augustus F. Hawkins issued a report critical of the series of studies published by Baker and de Kanter aimed at undermining bilingual education research. See Augustus F. Hawkins, Chair, Committee on Education and Labor in the House of Representatives. U.S., Congress, House, *A Report of the Compendium of Papers on the Topic of Bilingual Education of the Committee on Education and Labor,* 99th Congress, Second Sess. (Washington, D.C.: GPO, June, 1986). The following year the General Accounting Office (GAO) responded to Bennett's and Baker/de Kanter's charges of bilingual education's ineffectiveness and argued that the Education Department's primary conclusion about bilingual education—that native language instruction had been proven no more effective than "English-only" approaches—was unsupported by the research evidence cited by the department. See U.S. General Accounting Office, *Bilingual Education: A New Look at the Research Evidence* (Washington, D.C.: GPO, March 1987).

POLICY CONTINUATION, 1988–1994
Formation

A second aspect of Bennett's initiative was legislative reform. In March 1986 Secretary of Education William Bennett, in an effort to give local school districts more flexibility, formulated and introduced two bills into Congress: S. 2256 and HR 4538. These bills called for the elimination of the cap on funds for English-only instructional approaches in the 1984 bilingual bill and allowed funding of more alternatives to traditional bilingual education programs. The alternatives he supported included the use of English-only methods. In May and June of 1986 hearings were held by both houses on these bills. See U.S. House, Subcommittee on

Education, Arts, and Humanities of the Senate Labor and Human Resources Committee, *Hearings on S. 2256, A Bill to Amend the Bilingual Education Act,* 99th Congress, Second Sess. (Washington, D.C.: GPO, June 5, 1986).

For a brief summary of Bennett's presentation and the politics surrounding this bill see James Crawford, "Bennett Pushes Bilingual Bill in Congress," *Education Week,* 11 June 1986, 10, 14, and Judy Wiessler, "Hispanics blast effort to alter education plan," *Houston Chronicle,* 6 June 1986, 31. See also Crawford, *Bilingual Education: History, Politics, Theory, and Practice* (Trenton, NJ: Crane Publishing Company, 1989), 77–84, for further information on the passage of the 1988 bilingual bill and the compromises made by the Democrats and Republicans in order to enact this bill.

The bill was enacted in March 1988 and signed by Reagan in April of the same year. See The Bilingual Education Act of 1988, officially known as Public Law 100–297, 92 Stat. 279 (1988).

Implementation

1. Funding

When adjusted for inflation, the funding for bilingual education declined by seventy percent in the 1980s. Beginning in 1988, and at the urging of Reagan, twenty-five percent of bilingual education funds were earmarked for English immersion and alternative programs. See Nancy Mathis, "Study lauds bilingual education," *Houston Chronicle,* 12 February 1991, 1A.

2. Regulations

Several sets of regulations were developed during these years. See, for instance, the following: "Bilingual Education Programs," *Federal Register* 53, no. 193 (5 Oct. 1988): 39218–39224; "Notice of Proposed Priority," *Federal Register,* 55, no. 135 (13 July 1990): 28812; and "Bilingual Education Programs," *Federal Register* 58, no. 143 (28 July 1993): 40554–40560.

3. Implementation

During these years several different types of works focusing on general issues in implementing bilingual education were published. See for instance, Amado M. Padilla, Halford H. Fairchild, and Concepción M. Valadez, eds., *Bilingual Education: Issues and Strategies* (Newbury Park, CA: Sage Publications, 1990) and *A to EZ Handbook for Bilingual Teachers: Staff Development Guide* (NY: Macmillan/McGraw-Hill, 1993). A few specific issues occupied scholars interested in the implementation of bilingual education in the late 1980s and early 1990s. Among these were those pertaining to family and parental involvement, exiting bilingual programs, and effective practices in bilingual education. See, for instance, Heather McCollum and Alexander W. W. Russo, *Model Strategies in Bilingual Education: Family Literacy and Parent Involvement* (Washington, DC: U.S. Department of Education, 1993); Else V. Hamayan and Ron Perlman, *Helping Language Minority Students After They Exit from Bilingual/ESL Programs: A Handbook for Teachers* (Washington, DC: National Clearinghouse for Bilingual Education, 1990); and Choya L. Wilson, Patrick M. Shields, and Camille Marder, *The Title VII Academic Excellence Program: Disseminating Effective Programs and Practices in Bilingual Education* (Washington, DC: U.S. Dept of Education, Office of the Under Secretary, 1994).

4. Compliance

The federal government did not take any action, either for or against, existing bilingual programs but it sought to discredit the program or to undo the existing *Lau* agreements through legislative changes. (See formation stage, next policymaking cycle).

Evaluation/Impact

During these years several reports and studies supporting or criticizing bilingual education were published. The most important study critical of bilingual education was done by Rosale Pedalino Porter. Her study, a book titled *Forked Tongue: The Politics of Bilingual Education* (NY: Basic Books, 1990), argued that bilingual education was not working in assimilating

LEP children into American life. Bilingual education, she noted, fostered and prolonged ethnic segregation, robbed children of their chance to become full participants in American life, and contributed to the fragmentation of this nation into competing ethnic groups. These ideas of the fragmentation of American life and the failure to assimilate were reflected in other popular books such as Arthur M. Schlesinger, Jr., *The Disuniting of America* (New York: W.W. Norton, 1992) and William J. Bennett, *The Devaluing of America: The Fight for Our Culture and Our Children* (NY: Touchstone, 1992).

Other studies provided increasing support for bilingual education and began to show its effectiveness. Of particular importance were the results of a comprehensive study comparing the three most common methods of teaching LEP children. This study, commonly referred to as the Ramirez Report, showed the relative success of late-exit bilingual education over English-only methods. For an overview of this study and the praise for bilingual education by the George Bush administration, in contrast to the Reagan administration which opposed this program, see Nancy Mathis, "Study lauds bilingual education," *Houston Chronicle*, 12 February 1991, 1A. For more scholarly analysis of this report see Jim Cummins, "Bilingual Education and English Immersion: The Ramirez Report in Theoretical Perspective," *Bilingual Research Journal: The Journal of the National Association for Bilingual Education*, 16, 1–2 (Winter-Spring 1992): 91–104 and Wayne P. Thomas, "An Analysis of the Research Methodology of the Ramirez Study," *Bilingual Research Journal: The Journal of the National Association for Bilingual Education*, 16, 1–2 (Winter-Spring 1992): 213–245.

POLICY STALEMATE, 1994–2001
Formation

In 1993, one bill was introduced to repeal the Bilingual Education Act and to establish English as the country's official language. No action was taken on it. This bill was briefly discussed in William Pack, "Future appears secure for bilingual education," *Houston Post*, 27 February 1993, 13H.

Another bill to revise bilingual education was introduced in that same year. For a brief analysis of the congressional efforts to revise this policy see "Bilingual Education," *Congressional Quarterly Researcher* 3:30 (Aug 1993): 697–720. Despite tough financial times, pending funding battles in Washington and criticism from English-only advocates, proponents of bilingual education were optimistic that no significant changes in this policy would be made because of strong support from the public and President Clinton and his administration. For this optimistic view of bilingual legislative changes among advocates of bilingual education see William Pack, "Future appears secure," cited above.

A new bilingual education bill was enacted in September 1994. This bill (Title VII: Bilingual Education, Language Enhancement, and Language Acquisition Programs) was part of a larger omnibus education bill known as Improving America's Schools Act of 1994, Public Law 103–382, 108 Stat. 3519 (1994).

Implementation

1. Funding

Funding for bilingual education steadily increased during the 1990s despite cuts in federal education programs. Not all aspects of bilingual education received increased funding. In 1996, for instance, funding for bilingual educational instructional services grants increased over the prior year but both bilingual education support services and professional development programs were "zero-funded." For a brief overview of this funding development see Delia Pompa, Director, Office of Bilingual Education and Minority Languages Affairs, "Final Bilingual Education Budget Brings Mixed Blessings," *Fax-Newsletter,* October 2, 1996, 1. (in author's possession).

2. Regulations

For information on the regulations for implementing bilingual education programs see "Bilingual Education," *Federal Register* 60, no. 127 (3 July 1995): 34768–34769.

3. Implementation concerns

During these years, various forces affected the implementation of this bill, including the federal budget deficit, the changing nature of the political climate, English-only organizations, and increasing nativism at the state and local levels. Despite this changing political context, educators continued refining the implementation of bilingual education. For an overview of issues in implementing bilingual education programs during these years see Toni Griego-Jones, *Implementing Bilingual Programs is Everybody's Business* (Washington, DC: National Clearinghouse for Bilingual Education, 1995). See also Margarita Espino Calderon and Liliana Minaya-Rowe, *Designing and Implementing Two-Way Bilingual Programs: A Step-by-Step Guide for Administrators, Teachers, and Parents* (Thousand Oaks, CA: Corwin Press, 2003).

4. Compliance

The federal government did not take any action, either for or against, existing bilingual programs but it sought to void the consent decrees that encouraged the establishment of bilingual programs (See formation state, next policymaking cycle).

Evaluation/Impact

During the second half of the 1990s, the attacks against bilingual education became increasingly strident. The upsurge in opposition to bilingual education began in 1995 when Sen. Bob Dole, in his quest for the presidency, spoke before an American Legion national convention in Indianapolis. He warned his audience that "ethnic separatism" was a threat to American unity and called for making English the official language of the country. For a summary of his talk see David S. Broder, "Dole gives support to making English the official language," *Houston Chronicle*, 5 September 1995, 2A.

Several articles from the syndicated columnist Joan Beck supported Dole's criticism of bilingual education and in favor of an English-only policy. See Joan Beck, "Emphasize what unites U.S.-English," *Houston Chronicle*, 12 September 1995, 16A, and "English-only law would make a better America," *Houston Chronicle*, 9 March 1997, 3C. On more general ideological attacks on immigrants who spoke these different languages see Peter Brimelow, *Alien Nation: Common Sense About America's Immigration Disaster* (New York: Harper Perennial, 1996).

In the next several years, countless articles opposed to bilingual education appeared. Most of them opposed this program because it allegedly did not teach immigrant children English and because Latino parents opposed it. See, for instance, Douglas Lasken, "Best way to teach students English? End bilingual education," *Houston Chronicle*, 19 January 1998, 19A, and Jorge Amselle, "Texas' Bilingual Mandates Are a Disservice to All," *Houston Chronicle*, 24 March 1997, 19A, and Alan Bernstein, "Bilingual Debate Has Texas Twang/Most Texans Oppose Method that Takes Years," *Houston Chronicle*, 25 May 1998, 1A.

Scholarly articles opposed to bilingual education and in support of English-only methods also surfaced. See, for instance, C. Rossell and R. Baker, "The Educational Effectiveness of Bilingual Education," *Research in the Teaching of English* 30:1 (1996): 7–74, and Charles L. Glenn, *What Does the National Research Council Study Tell Us About Educating Language Minority Children?* (Amherst, MA: READ Institute, 1997). The former argues that bilingual education did not work, the latter interpreted the findings of the NRC report to mean that, despite a generation of research, "there is no evidence that there will be long-term advantages or disadvantages to teaching limited-English students in the native language." The supporters of bilingual education vigorously rejected this interpretation. They argued that "empirical results . . . support the theory underlying native language instruction." See Diane August and Kenji Hakuta, Letter to Rosalie Porter, READ Institute, cited in James Crawford, "Bilingual Education," 1998, *http://www.ourworld.compuserve.com/homepages/JWCRAWFORD/new.htm.*

Supporters of bilingual education responded to these strident attacks in the latter part of the 1990s. See, for instance, Stephen D. Krashen, *Under Attack: The Case Against Bilingual Education* (Culver City, CA: Language Education Associates, 1996); James Crawford, *At War with Diversity: U.S. Language Policy in an Age of Anxiety* (Buffalo, NY:

Multilingual Matters, 2000); James Crawford, "Ten Common Fallacies About Bilingual Education," ERIC Digest, November 1998, EDO-FL-98–10, *http://www.ourworld.compuserve.com/homepages/JWCRAWFORD/new.htm*; Jay Greene, *A Meta-Analysis of the Effectiveness of Bilingual Education* (Claremont, Calif: Tomás Rivera Center, 1998); and Stephen D. Krashen, *Condemned Without a Trial: Bogus Arguments Against Bilingual Education* (Westport, CT: Heinemann, 1999).

POLICY TRANSFORMATION: FROM BILINGUAL TO "ENGLISH-ONLY," 2001

Several pieces of legislation aimed at eliminating the federal bilingual education bill were introduced from 1995 to 2001. One of the most publicized was submitted by House Majority Whip Tom DeLay, R-TX. Known as the English for Children Act, this bill, introduced in April 1998, would have effectively ended federal funding for about 750 bilingual programs nationwide that allowed the teaching of immigrant children in their native language until they learned English. DeLay's bill was denounced by LULAC as well as Gene Green and Sheila Jackson, both members of Congress from the Houston area. For information on DeLay's bill see the following: Greg McDonald, "DeLay may press to let states end bilingual education/Bill would abolish federal mandate," *Houston Chronicle*, 25 March 1998, 2A; Greg McDonald, "DeLay to target bilingual classes/Bill would eliminate federal office funds," *Houston Chronicle*, 22 April 1998, 1A; Jo Ann Zuniga, Greg McDonald, staff, "DeLay's bill attacking bilingual education gathering opposition," Houston Chronicle, 25 April 1998, 35A. For a statement in support of DeLay's bill see Eric J. Stone, Director of Research, U.S. English, "Testimony Before the House Subcommittee on Early Childhood, Youth and Families, regarding H.R. 3892, The English Language Fluency Act," April 30, 1998. Found in *www.us-english.org/betestimony.htm*.

In the early months of the 1998 congressional session, other bills aimed at overhauling bilingual education policy were introduced. In September 1998, the House approved one of these. The bill, HR 3892—the English Language Fluency Act—did not win approval in the Senate since Congress adjourned a month after its passage. If enacted, it would have converted funding for bilingual and immigrant education programs to a block grant, placed a limit of three years in bilingual education, nullified all compliance agreements related to bilingual education between states or districts and the Department of Education, and changed the name of the Education Department's office of bilingual and minority-languages affairs to the Office of English-Language Acquisition. For information on this bill see Joetta L. Sack, "Bilingual education Legislation passes House," *Teacher Magazine on the Web*, September 16, 1998, 1, *http://www.teachermagazine.org/ew/vol-18/02biling.h18.*

In May of the following year, President Clinton and Secretary of Education Riley submitted a new bill aimed at reauthorizing both the bilingual education act as well as the larger Elementary and Secondary Education Act. This education bill was to expire on September 30, 1999. The proposed legislation, the Educational Excellence for All Children Act of 1999, addressed the issues of bilingual education for limited English proficient students within the context of this larger bill. For a brief view of this bill see "Proposed ESEA Reauthorization and Title VII, *National Clearinghouse on Bilingual Education Newsline*, May 29, 1999, *http://www.ncbe.gwu.edu/newsline/1999/05/28.htm*. Online text, summaries and analysis of the Educational Excellence for All Children Act of 1999 can be found through the Department of Education web site: *http://www.ed.gov/offices/OESE/ESEA.*

In early July 1999, the U.S. House of Representatives Subcommittee on Early Childhood, Youth and Families, which is within the House Education and Workforce Committee, held the only field hearing on the reauthorization of the ESEA and bilingual education in McAllen, Texas. The presenters, all supporters of bilingual education, in general argued that bilingual education had come under fire because of misconceptions, double standards and an ignorance of research that proved its effectiveness. For information on the presenters and the arguments made in this hearing see Allie Johnson, "Texas educators lobby to reauthorize bilingual education," *The McAllen Monitor*, 8 July 1999, N.p.; Cecilia Balli, "Educators push for bilingual education," *Express-News*, no date but possibly 8 July 1999. (Both articles were found in "Bilingual education file," Local History Room, La Retama Library, Corpus Christi, Texas.)

For additional comments on the proposed changes in bilingual education during the fall months of 1999 and on the responses by the supporters of this program see "NABE Action Alert: Title VII Reauthorization bill moves through house committee," E-mail from Michele Hewlett-Gomez to supporters of bilingual education, 3 October 1999, 1–3, and "NABE Action Alert: Update on Federal Legislation Impacting Language-Minority Children," E-mail from Michele Hewlett-Gomez to supporters of bilingual education, Sunday, October 17, 1999. (Both of these are in author's possession.)

In 2001, George W. Bush, a Republican, assumed the presidency. From the beginning of his administration, President Bush expressed his support for eliminating the federal preference for bilingual education and for supporting English-only methods for teaching LEP children. For Bush's proposals on bilingual education in particular and education in general see Erik W. Robelen, "Bush Plan: No Child Will Be left Behind—Democrats, GOP Agree in Principle on Federal Role," *Education Week,* 31 January 2001, 1, 24. For a view of these proposed changes see Mary Ann Zehr, "Bush Plan Could Alter Bilingual Education," *Education Week on the Web,* 21 February 2001. 1–6. *www.edweek.org/ew/ewstory.cfm?slug=23 biling.h20.*

During the next several months, the ESEA legislation made its way through Congress as two distinct bills—H.R. 1 in the House and S. 1 in the Senate. For NABE's views on this legislation in early August see *NABE Action Alert: Congress Appoints Conferees on Legislation Governing Federal Bilingual Education,* 2 August 2001, 1–7. (in author's possession). For a copy of the proposed bill see *No Child Left Behind, Title III,* August 3, 2001. *www.ed.gov/inits/nclb/part7.html.*

The Senate and House approved the education reform bill in December. For an overview of these developments see "House OKs School Reform Bill," *Houston Chronicle,* 14 Dec. 2001, 10A. This bill authorized $26.5 billion in federal spending for the 2002 fiscal year that began October 1, a roughly $7 billion increase over 2001. It set up a comprehensive testing system to identity failing schools and needy students. It also stipulated that failing schools would receive resources to get them back on track, and that students could be offered the option of transferring to another public school or could have tutoring or other supplemental services.

President Bush signed the No Child Left Behind Act in early January 2002. It can be found in U.S. Congress, House of Representatives, *No Child Left Behind Act of 2001, Conference Report to Accompany H.R. 1,* 107th Congress, 1st Session, Report 107–334. The bilingual education act is Title III (Language Instruction for Limited English Proficient and Immigrant Children) of this bill. See Public Law 107–110, 115 Stat. 1689 (2002).

For two different responses to the Elementary and Secondary Education Act in general and the bilingual education bill in particular by supporters of this program see National Council of La Raza, "Statement of Raul Yzaguirre on the Elementary and Secondary Education Act," December 14, 2001, 1–2 (in author's possession) and James Crawford, "Obituary: The Bilingual Education Act, 1968–2002." N.d., *http://www. ourworld.compuserve.com/homepages/JWCRAWFORD/new.htm.* The former praises the bipartisan approach to the enactment of this bill and does not critique the new bill but cautions that the changes need to be more effectively monitored by the federal government; the latter argues that the new bill dismantles the federal Title VII program and turns most funding decisions over to the states. See also Josué M. González, "Editor's Introduction: Bilingual Education and the Federal Role, If Any . . . ," *Bilingual Research Journal* 26:2 (Summer 2002): v–ix.

NOTES

1. James E. Anderson, *Public Policy-Making,* Third edition (New York: Holt, Rinehart and Winston, 1984).